The
Long-Flowering
Garden

PROFESSOR MARSHALL CRAIGMYLE

The Long-Flowering Garden

Over 500 plants for all seasons and interests

MetroBooks

CREDITS
Managing Editor: Charlotte Davies
Editor: Madeline Weston
Designers: John Heritage, Mark Holt
Indexer: Madeline Weston
Reproduction: Studio Tec, England
Printed in China

Acknowledgements
I am indebted to Samuel Dobie and Son, Seedsmen, Long Road, Paignton, Devon for allowing me to photograph their Trial Grounds.
I owe a huge debt of gratitude to the staff of Salamander Books, and to Ms Charlotte Davies in particular, for all their help.
I have to thank Ms Madeline Weston, of Norwich, for reading and correcting the proofs.
Finally, I also owe my wife a great debt of gratitude for tolerating being alone on many long winter evenings when I was in the next room on my computer, and for her constant help, advice, and encouragement.

CONTENTS

INTRODUCTION

I suspect that I am like most gardeners in that I look for a long display of flowers in my garden, and so avoid those plants that do not bloom for very long. For example, Caucasian peony (*Paeonia mlokosewitchii*) and Quamash (*Camasia quamash*) are both very attractive plants but have a flowering season of less than a week. Many Irises have the same brief flowering period and so for 360 days of the year add little visual interest to the garden. Information on the length of flowering times is much needed and can be difficult to come by, hence why I decided to present my long-flowering favorites in this book. In it I offer a selection of plants chosen for the length of their flowering seasons of anything from several weeks to several months, or even all year. The information is arranged in three sections: Perennials; Shrubs and Sub-shrubs; Annuals and Biennials. All three categories are made up of long-flowering plants, so whatever conditions prevail in your garden you can choose plants that will offer a long display.

The enthusiast who enjoys a blaze of color in summer can plant annuals or other bedding plants, but this may result in empty beds over winter unless the beds are planted in autumn with hardy spring-flowering plants such as Sweet William, Wallflowers, or Primulas. This method of gardening is hard work however and gives disappointing results in winter.

Many gardeners living busy lives favor planting methods that are less labor-intensive than this. Perennials and shrubs require less work and both types have many evergreen members. A garden with a large percentage of evergreens is not bleak and bare in winter, and if the plants are chosen primarily for their long flowering times, they can still be long-blooming in summer. All long-flowering evergreen perennials and shrubs are listed in the Appendices section (page 152).

The Appendices section features plants that have been grouped according to shared characteristics to make choosing the right plants even easier. It lists long-flowering plants that are allergenic, those that are low-allergen, poisonous plants, and drought-tolerant plants for readers who garden in dry regions. I hope you find the right ones for your garden.

Marshall Craigmyle

Cobaea scandens

More than 500 plants are featured in this book. Each entry is illustrated with a color picture of the plant *in situ* and the following information is given for every one:

1) Scientific name, family, and common name and category, such as biennial or shrub

2) Maximum height in imperial and metric measurements

3) Maximum spread in imperial and metric measurements

4) Aspect preferred

5) Soil type required

6) Hardiness zone (rating)

7) Propagation method(s)

8) The attributes of the plant, the nature of the flower, and the inflorescence (see below) and its flowering season

10) For shrubs, a pruning regime

The Royal Horticultural Society in the UK carries out extensive trials of all categories of plants and the accolade of the Award of Garden Merit is given to the most outstanding plants. A plant which has the Award of Garden Merit will have the letters A.G.M. after its name.

The positive attributes and drawbacks of each plant will be given, as listed here:

Attributes

- Aromatic foliage
- Attracts bees
- Attracts butterflies
- Can be dried
- Drought-tolerant
- Evergreen
- Good cut flower
- Handsome foliage
- Low allergen
- Scented flowers

Drawbacks

- Attracts slugs
- Divide regularly
- Highly allergenic
- Invasive
- Must deadhead
- Must not be moved
- Poisonous
- Prone to mildew
- Requires space
- Requires staking
- Seeds everywhere
- Short-lived
- Skin irritant

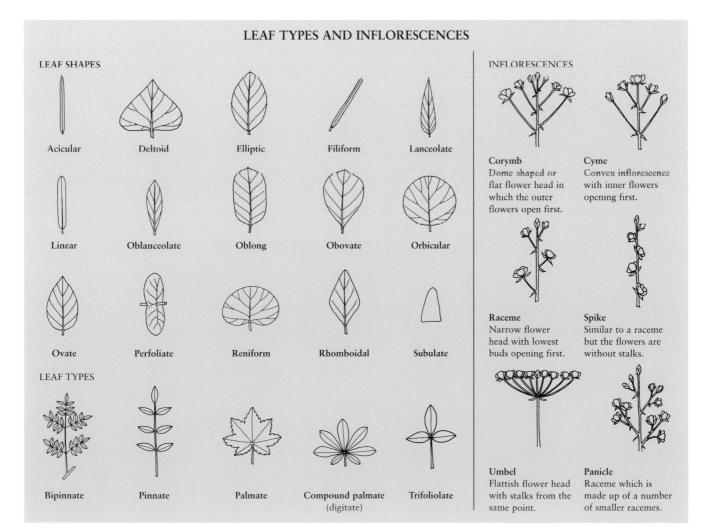

LEAF TYPES AND INFLORESCENCES

LEAF SHAPES

| Acicular | Deltoid | Elliptic | Filiform | Lanceolate |

| Linear | Oblanceolate | Oblong | Obovate | Orbicular |

| Ovate | Perfoliate | Reniform | Rhomboidal | Subulate |

LEAF TYPES

| Bipinnate | Pinnate | Palmate | Compound palmate (digitate) | Trifoliolate |

INFLORESCENCES

Corymb
Dome shaped or flat flower head in which the outer flowers open first.

Cyme
Convex inflorescence with inner flowers opening first.

Raceme
Narrow flower head with lowest buds opening first.

Spike
Similar to a raceme but the flowers are without stalks.

Umbel
Flattish flower head with stalks from the same point.

Panicle
Raceme which is made up of a number of smaller racemes.

HARDINESS ZONES

✸

The first consideration when choosing a perennial to be grown in the garden all year round is whether it is hardy in your area. The United States Department of Agriculture (USDA) has developed a system of temperature zones as a basis for assessing which plants can be grown in different areas. The zones are based on the annual average minimum temperature in an area, and are illustrated on the maps opposite and below of North America, Australia, New Zealand, South Africa, and Europe. The maps have been divided into the USDA climatic zones, numbered from Zone 1, the coldest, with a winter minimum of -50°F (-45°C), up to Zone 11, the warmest, with a minimum of +40°F (+5°C). Every entry in the directory section of this book cites the plant's hardiness zone. To establish whether a perennial will be hardy in your garden, refer to the map of hardiness zones and find the rating for your area. Any plant with a zonal rating equal to or lower than the rating for your area will be hardy in your garden. Thus if your area is rated Zone 7, all plants graded from Zone 1 to Zone 7 will survive and flower and plants graded Zone 8 to Zone 11 will not. However; Zone 8 plants may be grown outside provided they are given protection in the form of a deep mulch of bracken or leaves, a pane of glass, or a cloche, all of which keep the plants dry and help them substantially in surviving the winter. Zone 9 to Zone 11 plants can be grown out of doors in summer in a Zone 7 area, but will have to be lifted and kept under glass in winter or, alternatively, grown in containers and brought into a conservatory or greenhouse over winter.

Another consideration is that every garden has a number of microclimates – that is, some parts of the garden are warmer than others. It may be that the zonal rating for your area does not apply to all of your garden. So if your garden is rated Zone 7, the warmest corner, such as at the foot of a south-facing wall, may well be Zone 8. The only way to find out is to experiment by growing Zone 8-rated plants in that site.

TEMPERATURE RANGES

ZONE 1: Below -50°F (Below -45°C)
ZONE 2: -50 to -35°F (-45 to -37°C)
ZONE 3: -35 to -20°F (-37 to -29°C)
ZONE 4: -20 to -10°F (-29 to -23°C)
ZONE 5: -10 to -5°F (-23 to -21°C)
ZONE 6: -5 to 5°F (-21 to -15°C)
ZONE 7: 5 to 10°F (-15 to -12°C)
ZONE 8: 10 to 20°F (-12 to -7°C)
ZONE 9: 20 to 30°F (-7 to -1°C)
ZONE 10: 30 to 40°F (-1 to 4°C)
ZONE 11: Above +40°F (Above +5°C)

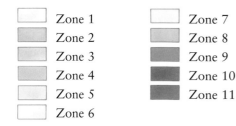

Zone 1
Zone 2
Zone 3
Zone 4
Zone 5
Zone 6
Zone 7
Zone 8
Zone 9
Zone 10
Zone 11

WESTERN EUROPE

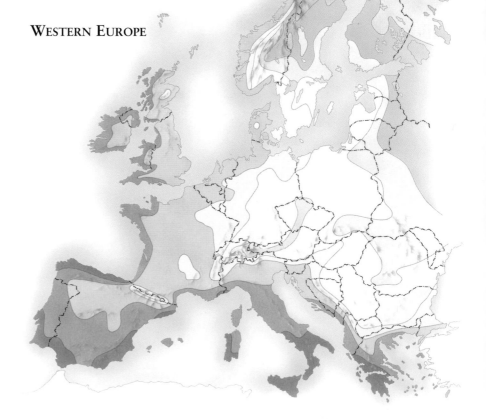

North America

The Southern Hemisphere

PERENNIALS

Perennials are non-woody plants that generally live for many years, given appropriate conditions. They may be evergreen but more commonly are herbaceous and die down to the ground in winter. Perennials are easy to cultivate, the most important requirement being good drainage. Those that are short-lived or require acid soil are highlighted in the text. Perennials vary widely in their degree of hardiness, from being hardy in all climates to being tender and incapable of being grown as perennials in unfavorable climates. Fortunately the majority fall into the hardy category and come through winters without requiring any special treatment. Consult the Hardiness Zones section before investing in plants, to ensure you choose plants that are hardy in your particular garden.

In cold climates, tender perennials can be sustained through the winter by insulating them: cover the crown of the plant with a thick surface mulch of garden compost, cork bark, coconut shell, or newspaper. Or cover with a glass cloche.

If your garden is in Zone 7, for example, you can overwinter Zone 8 plants by protecting them in these ways; however some plants will succumb to winter damp in very wet climates and sharp drainage may also be required.

Very tender perennials have to be brought into warmth in winter; they can be grown in containers, or the plants themselves lifted and brought indoors. Many tender perennials are treated as annuals and discarded at the end of the growing season. Flowers that seed in their first season and can be bought as seedlings in early spring should be planted out when all danger of frost is past. The plants are then disposed of when they die in the autumn frosts.

It is advisable, unless seed is required, to deadhead all perennials since the plants then divert energy into building up next season's growth rather than into setting seed. Some perennials have a long flowering season only if they are deadheaded regularly, and these are indicated in the text.

Acanthus spinosus A.G.M. (Acanthaceae)

Common name: None
Height: 5ft (1.5m)
Spread: 3ft (90cm)
Aspect: Sun or half shade
Soil: Fertile, deep, well-drained
Hardiness: Zone 6
Propagation: Seed in spring; division in spring or autumn
Flowering time: Late spring to midsummer

A clump-forming architectural evergreen perennial. Leaves spiny, deeply-cut, dark green. Flowers in racemes, soft mauve, with purple bracts.

- Drought-tolerant
- Evergreen
- Good cut flower
- Handsome foliage
- Low allergen

- Invasive
- Prone to mildew
- Requires staking
- Seeds everywhere

Acanthus spinosus A.G.M.

Aeonium cuneatum

Aeonium cuneatum (Crassulaceae)

Common name: None
Height: 6ft (1.8m)
Spread: 2ft (60cm)
Aspect: Half shade
Soil: Fertile; well drained
Hardiness: Zone 9
Propagation: Seed in warmth in spring; rosette cuttings in early summer
Flowering time: Spring and summer

A showy, evergreen, rosetted succulent. Spike-like panicles of yellow flowers.

- Evergreen
- Handsome foliage

Alcea rosea 'Chater's Double' group (Malvaceae)

Common name: Hollyhock
Height: 8ft (2.5m)
Spread: 2ft (60cm)
Aspect: Sun
Soil: Well-drained, fertile
Hardiness: Zone 3
Propagation: Seed, *in situ*, in summer
Flowering time: All summer

Very popular short-lived perennial. Leaves rounded, green, hairy. Flowers fully double in many shades. Requires staking. Hollyhock rust can be a problem: rust-proof strains exist.

- Attracts bees
- Low allergen

- Attracts slugs
- Requires staking
- Seeds everywhere
- Short-lived

Alchemilla mollis A.G.M. (Rosaceae)

Common name: Bear's-breech
Height: 2ft (60cm)
Spread: Almost indefinite
Aspect: Any
Soil: Any
Hardiness: Zone 3
Propagation: Seed in spring
Flowering time: All summer

A very common perennial. Leaves round, lobed, toothed, softly hairy, pale green. Flowers in small, greeny-yellow cymes.

- Drought-tolerant
- Good cut flower
- Handsome foliage

- Seeds everywhere

Alchemilla mollis A.G.M.

Alcea rosea 'Chater's Double' group

Alonsoa warzcewiczii A.G.M.

Alonsoa warzcewiczii A.G.M.
(Scrophulariaceae)

Common name: Heartleaf maskflower
Height: 2ft (60cm)
Spread: 1ft (30cm)
Aspect: Sun
Soil: Well-drained
Hardiness: Zone 10
Propagation: Seed, in warmth, in spring or autumn
Flowering time: All summer, into autumn

A red-stemmed perennial sub-shrub from Peru. Leaves ovate/lance, dark green. Flowers scarlet or white, spurred, in racemes. Best treated as an annual in cold climes.

● Good cut flower

ALSTROEMERIA *(Alstroemeriaceae)*
Alstroemeria

A genus of about 50 species of herbaceous perennials from mountains and grasslands of South America. They are tuberous-rooted, and clump up fairly rapidly; some members are invasive to a degree. The tubers are very friable and must be handled with care. Once planted (8in (20cm) deep) they should be left undisturbed. The foliage is linear/lance-shaped, green or gray-green, and may cause skin irritation. The flowers are 6 petaled funnels, borne in terminal 3- to 7-rayed umbels, on upright stems, and are ideal for cutting and universally handsome. The degree of hardiness varies from Zone 7 to Zone 9. A number of recently introduced hybrids are protected from being propagated without permission of the owner of the breeders' rights, and are marked PBR in the text . One such is the 'Princess' strain, which is dwarf and flowers all summer and autumn. Many of the other garden hybrids have a rather shorter flowering season. A list of hybrids not illustrated, but awarded the A.G.M. is given (see page 15).

Alstroemeria aurea

Alstroemeria aurea (Alstroemeriaceae)

Common name: None
Height: 3ft (90cm)
Spread: 18in (45cm)
Aspect: Sun or light shade
Soil: Well-drained, moist, fertile
Hardiness: Zone 7
Propagation: Seed when ripe; division in spring or autumn
Flowering time: Several weeks in summer

Tuberous. Leaves linear, mid-green. Flowers in terminal 3–7-rayed umbels, yellow-orange.

● Attracts bees   ● Attracts slugs
● Good cut flower   ● Highly allergenic
                         ● Invasive

Alstroemeria 'Endless Love' (PBR)
(Alstroemeriaceae)

Common name: None
Height: 1ft (30cm)
Spread: 18in (45cm)
Aspect: Sun or light shade
Soil: Well-drained, moist, fertile
Hardiness: Zone 7
Propagation: Division in spring or autumn
Flowering time: All summer, into autumn

Recent hybrid dwarf strain. Tuberous. Leaves linear/lance, mid-green. Flowers in terminal racemes, pink, purple spot. Choice.

● Attracts bees   ● Attracts slugs
● Good cut flower   ● Highly allergenic
                         ● Invasive

Alstroemeria ligtu hybrids A.G.M.
(Alstroemeriaceae)

Common name: None
Height: 3ft (90cm)
Spread: 18in (45cm)
Aspect: Sun or light shade
Soil: Moist, fertile, well-drained
Hardiness: Zone 7
Propagation: Seed when ripe; division, spring or autumn
Flowering time: All summer

Vigorous hybrids, which have been in our gardens for many years. Tuberous. Floppy unless staked. A wide range of colors from white through yellow, and orange to red.

● Attracts bees   ● Attracts slugs
● Good cut flower   ● Highly allergenic
                         ● Invasive
                         ● Must not be moved

Alstroemeria 'Endless Love' (PBR)

Alstroemeria Ligtu hybrids A.G.M.

Alstroemeria 'Pink Dream' (PBR)

Alstroemeria 'Princess Paola' ®

Alstroemeria psittacina

Alstroemeria 'Sunburst' (PBR)

Alstroemeria 'Pink Dream' (PBR) (Alstroemeriaceae)

Common name: None
Height: 1ft (30cm)
Spread: 18in (45cm)
Aspect: Sun, or light shade
Soil: Well-drained, fertile, moisture-retaining
Hardiness: Zone 8
Propagation: Division in spring or autumn
Flowering time: All summer and autumn

A recent dwarf hybrid. Tuberous. Flowers flesh-colored, with a prominent pink blotch and yellow throat.

- Attracts bees
- Good cut flower
- Attracts slugs
- Highly allergenic
- Must not be moved

Alstroemeria 'Princess Paola' ® (Alstroemeriaceae)

Common name: None
Height: 1ft (30cm)
Spread: 18in (45cm)
Aspect: Sun or very light shade
Soil: Well-drained, moisture-retentive
Hardiness: Zone 7
Propagation: Division, spring or autumn
Flowering time: All summer and autumn

A member of the highly floriferous and extremely long-flowering 'Princess' ® strain. Very choice, as are all this strain. May not be propagated without permission.

- Attracts bees
- Good cut flower
- Attracts slugs
- Highly allergenic
- Must not be moved

Alstroemeria psittacina (Alstroemeriaceae)

Common name: None
Height: 3ft (90cm)
Spread: 18in (45cm)
Aspect: Sun or light shade
Soil: Fertile, moisture-retentive, fertile
Hardiness: Zone 8
Propagation: Seed when ripe; division in spring or autumn
Flowering time: All summer

A species from Brazil. Stems spotted mauve. Flowers in umbels, green, overlaid dark red. Of interest, but not as spectacular as the hybrids.

- Attracts bees
- Good cut flower
- Attracts slugs
- Highly allergenic
- Must not be moved

Alstroemeria 'Sunburst' (PBR) (Alstroemeriaceae)

Common name: None
Height: 1ft (30cm)
Spread: 18in (45cm)
Aspect: Sun or light shade
Soil: Fertile, moisture-retentive, well-drained
Hardiness: Zone 8
Propagation: Division in spring or autumn
Flowering time: All summer, into autumn

Another very recent dwarf hybrid, with a new color break of rich plum purple. Tuberous. Very floriferous all summer and on into the autumn. Choice.

- Attracts bees
- Good cut flower
- Attracts slugs
- Highly allergenic
- Must not be moved

14

Alstroemeria 'Sunny Rebecca' (PBR)
(Alstroemeriaceae)

Common name: None
Height: 1ft (30cm)
Spread: 18in (45cm)
Aspect: Sun or light shade
Soil: Fertile, moisture-retentive, well-drained
Hardiness: Zone 8
Propagation: Division in spring or autumn
Flowering time: All summer and autumn

Another very recent dwarf hybrid. Tuberous. Handsome flowers of cream, blotched red, in cymes.

- Attracts bees
- Good cut flower
- Attracts slugs
- Highly allergenic
- Must not be moved

Alstroemeria 'Sweet Love' (PBR)
(Alstroemeriaceae)

Common Name: None
Height: 1ft (30cm)
Spread: 18in (45cm)
Aspect: Sun or light shade
Soil: Well-drained, moisture-retentive, fertile
Hardiness: Zone 8
Propagation: Division in spring or autumn
Flowering time: All summer, into autumn

A recent dwarf hybrid with very handsome flowers of a rich dark pink. Tuberous.

- Attracts bees
- Good cut flower
- Attracts slugs
- Highly allergenic
- Must not be moved

Alstroemeria 'Xandra' (PBR)
(Alstroemeriaceae)

Common name: None
Height: 1ft (30cm)
Spread: 18in (45cm)
Aspect: Sun or light shade
Soil: Fertile, well-drained, moisture-retentive
Hardiness: Zone 8
Propagation: Division in spring or autumn, should permission have been given
Flowering time: All summer, into autumn

A recent new dwarf hybrid with flowers of a striking orange, and with a yellow throat.

- Attracts bees
- Good cut flower
- Attracts slugs
- Highly allergenic
- Must not be moved

Alstroemeria 'Sunny Rebecca' (PBR)

Alstroemeria 'Sweet Love' (PBR)

Other Alstroemerias awarded the A.G.M. of the Royal Horticultural Society

'Apollo'
'Coronet'
'Friendship'
'H.R.H. Princess Alexandra'
'H.R.H Princess Alice' (PBR)
'Orange Gem'
'Orange Glory'
'Princess Carmina' ®
'Princess Caroline' ®
'Princess Grace' ® (PBR)
'Princess Juliana' ®
'Princess Mira' ® (PBR)
'Solent Crest'
'Solent Rose'
'Yellow Friendship'

Alstroemeria 'Xandra' (PBR)

ANEMONE (Ranunculaceae)
Anemone

A large genus of some 120 species, from a diverse range of habitats in both hemispheres, and, in addition, many hybrids exist. They may be spring-, summer- or autumn-flowering, and only the last group is long-flowering; they are fibrous-rooted, herbaceous, tall and grow in open sites in the wild. Some are poisonous, all are skin-irritant, and are prone to powdery mildew and slugs.

Anemone hupehensis var. *Japonica* 'Prinz Heinrich' A.G.M. (Ranunculaceae)

Common name: Dwarf Japanese anemone
Height: 3ft (90cm)
Spread: 16in (40cm)
Aspect: Sun or half shade
Soil: Humus-rich, fertile, moist
Hardiness: Zone 6
Propagation: Division, in spring or autumn
Flowering time: Mid and late summer

A fibrous-rooted, suckering hybrid. Leaves basal, oval, tripalmate, deep green. Flowers in umbels, petals dark pink.

- Attracts bees
- Good cut flower
- Attracts slugs
- Invasive
- Prone to mildew
- Skin irritant

Anemone multifida (Ranunculaceae)

Common name: None
Height: 1ft (30cm)
Spread: 6in (15cm)
Aspect: Sun or half shade
Soil: Humus-rich, moist, well-drained
Hardiness: Zone 2
Propagation: Seed, when ripe
Flowering time: Late summer, early autumn

A vigorous, rhizomatous species from N. America. Leaves rounded, palmate, basal and stem. Flowers in umbels of 2–3 creamy-white saucers.

- Good cut flower
- Handsome foliage
- Attracts slugs
- Prone to mildew
- Skin irritant

Anemone multifida

Anthemis marschalliana

ANTHEMIS (Asteraceae)
Anthemis

A genus of some 100 species from the Old World, Europe, and Eurasia in particular. They are extremely useful garden plants, undemanding, long-flowering, and have handsome, aromatic foliage. Their main drawback is that they are generally short-lived; their life can be extended by shearing them over immediately after flowering in order to encourage fresh basal shoots, which will help the plant to over-winter. They do not transplant well, but benefit nevertheless from regular division in spring. The flowers are daisy-like, and may have yellow or white ray florets, and all have a yellow disc. Some types are good for cutting. They are drought-tolerant.

Anthemis marschalliana ssp. biebersteiniana (Asteraceae)

Common name: None
Height: 18in (45cm)
Spread: 2ft (60cm)
Aspect: Full sun
Soil: Sharply-drained
Hardiness: Zone 7
Propagation: Seed, or division, in spring
Flowering time: Late spring to early summer

A mat-forming species from Turkey. Leaves obovate, bi-pinnatisect, gray, silky, aromatic. Yellow composite solitary flowers; leafy stems.

- Aromatic foliage
- Drought-tolerant
- Handsome foliage
- Attracts slugs
- Must not be moved
- Short-lived

Anemone hupehensis

Anthemis punctata ssp. *cupaniana* A.G.M.

Anthemis punctata ssp. *cupaniana* A.G.M.
(Asteraceae)

Common name: Dog fennel
Height: 1ft (30cm)
Spread: 3ft (90cm)
Aspect: Full sun
Soil: Sharply-drained
Hardiness: Zone 6
Propagation: Seed, or division, or basal
cuttings in spring
Flowering time: Early to midsummer

A handsome evergreen from Italy, with
aromatic, pinnatisect, silvery foliage.
Flowers are composites, white, long-lasting.

● Aromatic foliage
● Drought-tolerant
● Evergreen
● Good cut flower
● Handsome foliage

● Attracts slugs
● Must not be moved
● Prone to mildew
● Short-lived

Anthemis tinctoria 'E.C. Buxton'

Anthemis tinctoria 'E.C. Buxton'
(Asteraceae)

Common name: Golden marguerite, Ox-eye
Height: 28in (70cm)
Spread: 2ft (60cm)
Aspect: Full sun
Soil: Sharply-drained
Hardiness: Zone 6
Propagation: Division, or basal cuttings, in
spring
Flowering time: From late spring onwards

A handsome cultivar; lemon-yellow flowers.

● Aromatic foliage
● Drought-tolerant
● Evergreen
● Good cut flower
● Handsome foliage

● Attracts slugs
● Must not be moved
● Prone to mildew
● Short-lived

Anthemis tinctoria 'Sauce Hollandaise'
(Asteraceae)

Common name: Golden marguerite, Ox-eye
Height: 2ft (60cm)
Spread: 2ft (60cm)
Aspect: Full sun
Soil: Sharply-drained
Hardiness: Zone 6
Propagation: Division, or basal cuttings, in
spring
Flowering time: Late spring to late summer

An extremely handsome cultivar, with
flowers of palest cream, bordering on white.

● Aromatic foliage
● Drought-tolerant
● Evergreen
● Good cut flower
● Handsome foliage

● Attracts slugs
● Must not be moved
● Prone to mildew
● Short-lived

Anthemis tinctoria 'Sauce Hollandaise'

Antirrhinum majus 'Floral Showers' series
(Scrophulariaceae)

Common name: Common snapdragon
Height: 8in (20cm)
Spread: 1ft (30cm)
Aspect: Full sun
Soil: Sharply-drained, fertile
Hardiness: Zone 7
Propagation: Seed in spring or autumn
Flowering time: All summer

A short-lived perennial, grown almost
always as an annual. Leaves lance-shaped,
glossy green. Flowers in a wide range of
colors. Must be deadheaded regularly.

● Good cut flower
● Low allergen
● Scented flowers

● Must deadhead
● Prone to mildew
● Seeds everywhere
● Short-lived

Antirrhinum majus 'Sonnet' series
(Scrophulariaceae)

Common name: Common snapdragon
Height: 18in (45cm)
Spread: 10in (25cm)
Aspect: Sun
Soil: Sharply-drained, fertile
Hardiness: Zone 7
Propagation: Seed in spring or autumn
Flowering time: All summer

A short-lived perennial, grown almost
invariably as an annual. Flowers in a wide
color range; must be deadheaded.

● Good cut flower
● Low allergen

● Must deadhead
● Prone to mildew
● Seeds everywhere
● Short-lived

Antirrhinum majus 'Floral Showers'

Antirrhinum majus 'Sonnet' series

Arctotis x *hybrida*

Aster x *frikartii* 'Flora's Delight'

Arctotis x *hybrida* (Asteraceae)

Common name: African daisy
Height: 2ft (60cm)
Spread: 1ft (30cm)
Aspect: Full sun
Soil: Moist, well-drained.
Hardiness: Zone 9
Propagation: Seed in heat, in spring or autumn
Flowering time: All summer and autumn

A very handsome composite, from S. Africa. Leaves felted, often silver, elliptic, wavy-edged. Flowers solitary; colors from white through yellow, orange to pink or red.

- Handsome foliage
- Highly allergenic
- Must deadhead

Aster x *frikartii* 'Flora's Delight' (Asteraceae)

Common name: None
Height: 20in (50cm)
Spread: 1ft (30cm)
Aspect: Sun or part shade
Soil: Moist, fertile
Hardiness: Zone 2
Propagation: Division, in spring
Flowering time: Late summer to mid-autumn.

A dense, bushy, hardy perennial. Leaves gray-green. Flowers in loose corymbs, lilac, very long-lasting.

- Attracts butterflies
- Attracts slugs
- Good cut flower
- Highly allergenic

Aster x *frikartii* 'Monch' A.G.M. (Asteraceae)

Common name: None
Height: 28in (70cm)
Spread: 16in (40cm)
Aspect: Sun or half shade
Soil: Moist, fertile
Hardiness: Zone 2
Propagation: Division in spring
Flowering time: Late summer to early autumn

Hardy perennial. Leaves ovate/oblong, rough, deep green. Flowers very long-lasting, violet-blue with orange discs.

- Attracts butterflies
- Attracts slugs
- Good cut flower
- Highly allergenic

Aster x *frikartii* 'Monch' A.G.M.

Aster sedifolius 'Nanus' (Asteraceae)

Common name: None
Height: 18in (45cm)
Spread 18in (45cm)
Aspect: Sun or part shade
Soil: Moist, fertile
Hardiness: Zone 6
Propagation: Seed or division, in spring
Flowering time: Late summer to early autumn

A compact, dwarf, hardy perennial. Flowers daisy-like, dark blue, with yellow centers, very long-lasting.

- Attracts butterflies
- Attracts slugs
- Good cut flower
- Highly allergenic

Aster sedifolius 'Nanus'

Aster thomsonii 'Nanus' (Asteraceae)

Common name: None
Height: 18in (45cm)
Spread: 10in (25cm)
Aspect: Sun or part shade
Soil: Moist, fertile
Hardiness: Zone 7
Propagation: Seed, or division, in spring or autumn
Flowering time: Late summer to mid-autumn.

A compact, dwarf hardy perennial. Flowers star-shaped, lilac-blue, long-lasting, in terminal sprays.

- Attracts butterflies
- Good cut flower
- Attracts slugs
- Highly allergenic

Aster thomsonii 'Nanus'

BEGONIA (Begoniaceae)
Begonia

A huge genus of some 500 species, from subtropical and tropical regions of both hemispheres. As a consequence, the vast majority are graded Zone 10 as far as hardiness is concerned as are the innumerable hybrids in cultivation. *Begonia grandis* ssp. evansiana, at Zone 8, is the only hardy member of the genus, and *Begonia sutherlandii* is Zone 9.

Begonias may be tuberous- or fibrous-rooted, or rhizomatous. All have both male and female flowers on the same plant, and indeed on the same inflorescence, which is either a raceme or a cyme; female flowers have between 2 and 6 petals of equal size, whereas male flowers have between 2 and 4 petals of unequal size. The classification of the genus is complex, but 'The Plant Finder' recognizes the following categories:

Cane (C) Woody, evergreen, hybrid perennials derived mainly from Brazilian species. This category includes members grown for foliage value, and others for flowers, which appear from early spring to summer. They have bamboo-like stems. They will not tolerate direct sunlight all day.

Rex (R) This group is grown for foliage value alone, since the flowers are inconspicuous. They are derived from crosses with *Begonia rex* as one parent. They are not included here.

Semperflorens Cultorum (S) Fibrous-rooted, compact, evergreen, hybrid perennials derived from several species; they may be grown for foliage or flowers, which appear all summer long. They do well in part-shade, and are not very tolerant of direct sunlight.

x tuberhybrida (T) Tuberous winter-dormant perennials, derived from Andean species. They may be upright or pendulous, having succulent stems, and most of them are summer-flowering. The flowering spike has one large (sometimes double) male flower and two small female ones.

Begonia grandis ssp. evansiana (T) (Begoniaceae)

Common name: Evans begonia
Height: 32in (80cm)
Spread: 1ft (30cm)
Aspect: Sun or part shade
Soil: Moist, moisture-retentive
Hardiness: Zone 8
Propagation: Separate tubers, in autumn
Flowering time: All summer

A hardy tuberous species. Leaves ovate, pointed, olive-green. Flowers, pink, scented in pendent cymes on tallish, branched stems.

- Drought-tolerant
- Handsome foliage
- Scented flowers
- Prone to mildew
- Seeds everywhere

Begonia grandis ssp. *evansiana*

Begonia x tuberhybrida 'Non-stop' series

Common name: Tuberous begonia
Height: 1ft (30cm)
Spread: 1ft (30cm)
Aspect: Part-shade, no midday sun
Soil: Moisture-retentive, moist
Hardiness: Zone 10
Propagation: Seed in spring; basal or side-shoot cuttings in summer
Flowering time: All summer

An upright, compact series with leaves of mid-green, heart-shaped. Flowers solitary, double, of red, yellow, pink, white or orange. Lift tubers before first frost, and dry off.

- Handsome foliage
- Low allergen

Begonia x tuberhybrida 'Non-stop' series

Begonia semperflorens 'Cocktail' series A.G.M. (S) (Begoniaceae)

Common name: Wax begonia
Height: 1ft (30cm)
Spread: 1ft (30cm)
Aspect: Half shade, or protection from midday sun
Soil: Well-drained, moisture-retentive
Hardiness: Zone 10
Propagation: Division in spring
Flowering time: All summer

A very popular bedding plant, once all danger of frost is past. Leaves rounded, bright green. Flowers weather-resistant, single, in a wide range of colors, including bicolors. Lift tubers in autumn before frost and dry off.

● Handsome foliage
● Low allergen

Begonia sutherlandii A.G.M. (T) (Begoniaceae)

Common name: Sutherland begonia
Height: 6in (15cm)
Spread: 20in (50cm)
Aspect: Part-shade, or protection from midday sun
Soil: Well-drained, moisture-retentive
Hardiness: Zone 9
Propagation: Seed in spring: basal or side-shoot cuttings in summer
Flowering time: All summer

A tuberous begonia from S. Africa. Leaves ovate/lance, bright green. Stems trailing. Flowers in pendent panicles, orange.

● Handsome foliage
● Low allergen

Bellis perennis 'Pomponette' series A.G.M. (Asteraceae)

Common name: None
Height: 8in (20cm)
Spread: 8in (20cm)
Aspect: Sun or part shade
Soil: Well-drained
Hardiness: Zone 4
Propagation: Seed or division in spring
Flowering time: Late winter to late summer

A clone in which the flower heads are fully double, and may be white, pink, or red; the petals are quilled. Leaves dull green, spoon-shaped, in basal rosettes. Evergreen. Good ground cover. Deadhead to prevent seeding.

● Evergreen   ● Highly allergenic
● Good cut flower   ● Seeds everywhere

Bidens ferulifolia A.G.M. (Asteraceae)

Common name: Beggar-ticks
Height: 1ft (30cm)
Spread: Indefinite
Aspect: Full sun
Soil: Moist, well-drained
Hardiness: Zone 8
Propagation: Seed in heat in spring
Flowering time: Mid-spring to late autumn

A short-lived perennial, grown usually as an annual. Leaves tripinnate, green, the lobes lance-shaped. Flowers daisy-like, single, yellow, on spreading stems. Good in hanging baskets.

● Short-lived

Borago pygmaea (Boraginaceae)

Common name: None
Height: 2ft (60cm)
Spread: 2ft (60cm)
Aspect: Part shade
Soil: Moist
Hardiness: Zone 7
Propagation: Seed in situ in spring
Flowering time: Early summer to early autumn

Leaves in basal rosettes, ovate, rough, green. Flowers in cymes, bell-shaped, clear blue.

● Prone to mildew
● Seeds everywhere
● Short-lived

Begonia semperflorens 'Cocktail' series

Begonia sutherlandii A.G.M.

Bellis perennis 'Pomponette' series A.G.M.

Bidens ferulifolia A.G.M.

Borago pygmaea

Bracteantha 'Coco'

Buphthalmum salicifolium

Bracteantha 'Coco' (Asteraceae)

Common name: None
Height: 2ft (60cm)
Spread: 1ft (30cm)
Aspect: Shade
Soil: Sharply-drained, fertile
Hardiness: Zone 8
Propagation: Division in spring
Flowering time: Summer to mid-winter

An 'everlasting' short-lived perennial. Leaves ovate, mid-green. Flowers off-white, papery. Grow in dry shade.

- Can be dried
- Drought-tolerant
- Short lived

Buphthalmum salicifolium (Asteraceae)

Common Name: Willowleaf-oxeye
Height: 2ft (60cm)
Spread: 18in (45cm)
Aspect: Full sun
Soil: Dry, gritty, poor
Hardiness: Zone 4
Propagation: Seed or division, in spring
Flowering time: All summer

A little-known gem. Leaves narrow, obovate, deep green. Flowers daisy-like, bright yellow, on long erect stems. Trouble-free.

- Good cut flower
- Highly allergenic

Calceolaria biflora

Calceolaria biflora (Scrophulariaceae)

Common name: Slipperflower, Slipperwort
Height: 10in (25cm)
Spread: 8in (20cm)
Aspect: Sun or part shade
Soil: Acid, fertile, gritty
Hardiness: Zone 6
Propagation: Seed, or division, in spring
Flowering time: All summer

A rhizomatous, evergreen, mat-forming perennial. Leaves in rosettes, oblong, toothed, dark green. Flowers two-lipped, yellow, in loose racemes of up to eight.

- Evergreen
- Drought-tolerant
- Attracts slugs

Calceolaria 'Sunset Red' (Scrophulariaceae)

Common name: None
Height: 1ft (30cm)
Spread: 1ft (30cm)
Aspect: Sun or part shade
Soil: Acid, gritty, fertile
Hardiness: Zone 9
Propagation: Seed or division, in spring
Flowering time: Mid-spring to midsummer

An evergreen, compact, bushy, perennial. Leaves ovate/lance, gray-green. Flowers pouched, red. Comes in yellow, orange or bicolored forms. Best treated as an annual in cold areas.

- Evergreen
- Attracts slugs

Calceolaria 'Sunset Red'

CAMPANULA (Campanulaceae)
Campanula

A genus of some 300 species of annuals, biennials, and perennials from a variety of habitats in temperate zones of the northern hemisphere, and Turkey and south Europe in particular: their cultural needs vary therefore. They are, in general, undemanding, and bloom from late spring to late summer. The flowers may be bell- or star-shaped, or tubular. Most are well-behaved, but some (CC. pulla, persicifolia, and takesimana in particular) are rampant invaders, and C. persicifolia also seeds everywhere. Some are prone to powdery mildew, and all are slug prone.

Campanula carpatica A.G.M. (Campanulaceae)

Common name: Carpathian bellflower
Height: 8in (20cm)
Spread: 2ft (60cm)
Aspect: Sun or part shade
Soil: Moist, well-drained
Hardiness: Zone 3
Propagation: Seed in autumn
Flowering time: Several weeks in summer

A clump-forming perennial. Leaves basal, ovate, toothed, mid-green. Flowers solitary, upturned bells, violet, or blue or white.

● Good cut flower　　● Attracts slugs

Campanula glomerata 'Superba' A.G.M. (Campanulaceae)

Common name: Clustered bellflower
Height: 2ft (60cm)
Spread: Indefinite
Aspect: Sun or half shade
Soil: Moist, well-drained, alkaline
Hardiness: Zone 3
Propagation: Seed, in spring
Flowering time: All summer

A vigorous perennial. Leaves lance-shaped, toothed, dark green. Flowers in terminal racemes, bell-shaped, purple-violet.

● Attracts bees　　● Attracts slugs
● Good cut flower

Campanula carpatica A.G.M.

Campanula lactiflora (Campanulaceae)

Common name: Milky bellflower
Height: 5ft (1.5m)
Spread: 2ft (60cm)
Aspect: Sun or half shade
Soil: Moist, well-drained, alkaline, fertile
Hardiness: Zone 5
Propagation: Seed in spring
Flowering time: Early summer to early autumn

A vigorous, upright perennial. Leaves ovate, toothed, mid-green. Flowers in conical panicles, open bells, white, blue, or lavender. Will repeat-flower if deadheaded.

● Attracts bees　　　● Attracts slugs
● Good cut flower　　● Must not be moved
　　　　　　　　　　● Requires staking
　　　　　　　　　　● Seeds everywhere

Campanula latiloba 'Hidcote Amethyst' A.G.M. (Campanulaceae)

Common name: None
Height: 3ft (90cm)
Spread: 18in (45cm)
Aspect: Sun or part shade
Soil: Moist, well-drained, alkaline, fertile
Hardiness: Zone 3
Propagation: Division in spring or autumn
Flowering time: Mid and late summer

A handsome clone of a Turkish species. Leaves basal, lance-shaped, toothed, green. Flowers cup-shaped, pale amethyst, in racemes.

● Attracts bees　　　● Attracts slugs
● Good cut flower

Campanula lactiflora

Campanula latiloba 'Hidcote Amethyst'

Campanula glomerata 'Superba' A.G.M.

Campanula persicifolia 'Blue Bloomers'
(Campanulaceae)

Common name: Peach-leaved bellflower
Height: 3ft (90cm)
Spread: 1ft (30cm)
Aspect: Sun or part shade
Soil: Well-drained, moist, alkaline, fertile
Hardiness: Zone 3
Propagation: Division in spring or autumn
Flowering time: Early and midsummer

A handsome clone of this popular plant.
Flowers in racemes, lilac-blue. Will repeat-
flower if sheared over after flowering.

- Attracts bees
- Evergreen
- Good cut flower
- Low allergen
- Attracts slugs
- Divide regularly
- Invasive
- Requires staking
- Seeds everywhere

CANNA *(Cannaceae)*
Canna

A genus of some 50 species, but of
hundreds of hybrids which are
sometimes grouped under the names,
Canna generalis or *Canna orchiodes*.
The have large paddle-shaped leaves,
pinnately-veined, and usually green, but
may be purple; they can be handsomely-
striated in some clones. The asymmetric
flowers are borne in racemes or
panicles, and are usually paired in the
leaf axils. They are brightly-colored, and
the flowering season is long, especially if
deadheaded. Unfortunately they are not
especially weather-resistant, nor are they
very hardy, so in cold areas must be
given winter protection, or the rhizomes
can be lifted and stored in frost-free
conditions.
   Cannas like full sun, good drainage,
and fertile soil, but plenty of water
during the growing season. They do not
require to be staked except in very
exposed sites. They are trouble-free,
except that they are prone to attack by
slugs. They are low-allergen plants, and
make good cut flowers.

Canna 'Assault' (Cannaceae)

Common name: None
Height: 6ft (1.8m)
Spread: 20in (50cm)
Aspect: Full sun
Soil: Well-drained, fertile
Hardiness: Zone 8
Propagation: Division in spring
Flowering time: Midsummer to autumn

A tuberous perennial. Leaves large, paddle-
shaped, purple-brown. Flowers in racemes,
orange-scarlet, like gladioli.

- Good cut flower
- Handsome foliage
- Low allergen
- Attracts slugs
- Must deadhead

Canna 'Champion' (Cannaceae)

Common name: None
Height: 4ft (1.2m)
Spread: 20in (50cm)
Aspect: Sun
Soil: Well-drained, fertile
Hardiness: Zone 8
Propagation: Division in spring
Flowering time: Midsummer to mid-autumn

A half-hardy tuberous perennial. Leaves
large, paddle-shaped, mid-green. Flowers
gladiolus-like, in racemes, red.

- Good cut flower
- Handsome foliage
- Low allergen
- Attracts slugs
- Must deadhead

Canna 'En Avant' (Cannaceae)

Common name: None
Height: 5ft (1.5m)
Spread: 2ft (60cm)
Aspect: Full sun
Soil: Well-drained, fertile
Hardiness: Zone 8
Propagation: Division in spring
Flowering time: Midsummer to mid-autumn

A tuberous perennial. Leaves very large,
paddle-shaped, mid-green. Flowers in
racemes, like gladioli, yellow, streaked brown.

- Good cut flower
- Handsome foliage
- Low allergen
- Attracts slugs
- Must deadhead

Canna 'En Avant'

Campanula persicifolia 'Blue Bloomers'

Canna 'Champion'

Canna 'Fireside'

Canna 'Hercule'

Canna 'Rosemond Coles'

Catharanthus roseus

Canna 'Rosemond Coles' (Cannaceae)

Common name: None
Height: 4ft (1.2m)
Spread: 20in (50cm)
Aspect: Full sun
Soil: Well-drained, fertile
Hardiness: Zone 8
Propagation: Division in spring
Flowering time: Midsummer to autumn

A tuberous perennial. Leaves large, paddle-shaped, bright green, veined cream. Flowers in racemes, like gladioli, scarlet, edged yellow.

- Good cut flower
- Handsome foliage
- Low allergen
- Attracts slugs
- Must deadhead

Canna 'Taroudant' (Cannaceae)

Common name: None
Height: 4ft (1.2m)
Spread: 2ft (60cm)
Aspect: Full sun
Soil: Well-drained, fertile
Hardiness: Zone 8
Propagation: Division of tubers in spring
Flowering time: Midsummer to mid-autumn

A tender, tuberous perennial. Leaves large, paddle-shaped, green. Flowers yellow, suffused and blotched orange, in racemes.

- Good cut flower
- Handsome foliage
- Low allergen
- Attracts slugs
- Must deadhead

Canna 'Fireside' (Cannaceae)

Common name: None
Height: 4ft (1.2m)
Spread: 20in (50cm)
Aspect: Full sun
Soil: Well-drained, fertile
Hardiness: Zone 8
Propagation: Division in spring
Flowering time: Midsummer to mid-autumn

A tender, tuberous perennial. Leaves large, paddle-shaped, green. Flowers in racemes, red with a yellow throat.

- Good cut flower
- Handsome foliage
- Low allergen
- Attracts slugs
- Must deadhead

Catharanthus roseus (Apocynaceae)

Common name: None
Height: 2ft (60cm)
Spread: 2ft (60cm)
Aspect: Sun
Soil: Well-drained, fertile
Hardiness: Zone 10
Propagation: Seed in heat in spring
Flowering time: Spring to summer

A tender, evergreen perennial, usually grown as an annual in cold areas. Flowers salverform, pink, red or white in the upper leaf axils.

- Drought-tolerant
- Evergreen
- Poisonous

Canna 'Hercule' (Cannaceae)

Common name: None
Height: 4ft (1.2m)
Spread: 2ft (60cm)
Aspect: Sun
Soil: Well-drained, fertile
Hardiness: Zone 8
Propagation: Division of tubers in spring
Flowering time: Midsummer to mid-autumn

A tender, tuberous perennial. Leaves large, paddle-shaped, bronze. Flowers in racemes, bright red.

- Good cut flower
- Handsome foliage
- Low allergen
- Attracts slugs
- Must deadhead

Canna 'Taroudant'

Celosia argentea 'Fairy Fountains'
(Amaranthaceae)

Common mame: None
Height: 2ft (60cm)
Spread: 18in (45cm)
Aspect: Full sun
Soil: Moist, well-drained, fertile
Hardiness: Zone 9
Propagation: Seed in heat in spring
Flowering time: All summer

Grown as an annual in cold regions. Leaves
lance-shaped, pale green. Inflorescence
plume-like, in terminal feathery pyramidal
cymes of tiny flowers, pink, cream, or red.

- Can be dried
- Good cut flower

Centranthus ruber (Valerianaceae)

Common name: Red valerian
Height: 3ft (90cm)
Spread: 3ft (90cm)
Aspect: Sun
Soil: Poor, well-drained, alkaline
Hardiness: Zone 7
Propagation: Seed in spring
Flowering time: Late spring to late summer

A common weed of dry, stony places. Leaves
ovate, fleshy, glaucous. Flowers small,
perfumed, red (or pink or white) in dense
cymes. Cut back after flowering to prevent
self-seeding.

- Attracts bees   - Must not be moved
- Drought-tolerant   - Seeds everywhere
- Good cut flower
- Scented flowers

Chrysogonum virginianum (Asteraceae)

Common name: Goldenstar
Height: 10in (25cm)
Spread: 10in (25cm)
Aspect: Sun or part shade
Soil: Moist, well-drained, humus-rich
Hardiness: Zone 5
Propagation: Seed when ripe; division in
spring or autumn
Flowering time: Early spring to late summer

A creeping, rhizomatous, evergreen
perennial from eastern U.S.A. Leaves ovate,
hairy, green. Flowers solitary, star-shaped,
5-petaled, yellow.

- Evergreen

Clematis x *eriostemon* 'Hendersonii'
(Ranunculaceae)

Common name: None
Height: 9ft (2.7m)
Spread: 3ft (90cm)
Aspect: Any
Soil: Well-drained, fertile, humus-rich
Hardiness: Zone 4
Propagation: Division, basal or softwood
cuttings, all in spring
Flowering time: Summer and autumn

A small-flowered, late-flowering, scandent
species. Flowers bell-shaped, nodding,
purple-blue, with creamy-yellow anthers.
Prune in spring to 6in (15cm) from ground.

- Attracts bees   - Prone to mildew
- Low allergen   - Skin irritant

Celosia argentea 'Fairy Fountains'

Centranthus ruber

Clematis x *eriostemon* 'Hendersonii'

Chrysogonum virginianum

Cobaea scandens A.G.M.

Convolvulus althaeoides

Convolvulus sabatius A.G.M.

Convolvulus tricolor 'Royal Ensign'

Cobaea scandens A.G.M. (Polemoniaceae)

Common name: Cup-and-saucer vine
Height: 70ft (21m)
Spread: 3ft (90cm)
Aspect: Full sun
Soil: Moist, well-drained, fertile
Hardiness: Zone 9
Propagation: Seed in heat in spring; softwood cuttings, with bottom heat, in summer
Flowering time: Summer to autumn

A robust, upright, evergreen, semi-woody perennial climber; usually grown as an annual. Flowers scented, bell-shaped, green becoming purple.

- Evergreen
- Scented flowers
- Requires space

Convolvulus althaeoides (Convolvulaceae)

Common name: Bindweed
Height: 1ft (30cm)
Spread: Indefinite
Aspect: Full sun
Soil: Well-drained
Hardiness: Zone 8
Propagation: Seed in heat, in spring
Flowering time: Mid to late summer

An invasive trailing perennial which can be trained upwards. Leaves silver-green. Flowers clear pink saucers. Grow in a container sunk in the ground.

- Drought-tolerant
- Invasive

Convolvulus sabatius A.G.M. (Convolvulaceae)

Common name: Bindweed
Height: 6in (15cm)
Spread: 2ft (60cm)
Aspect: Full sun
Soil: Well-drained
Hardiness: Zone 8
Propagation: Seed in heat, or softwood cuttings, in spring
Flowering time: Summer to early autumn

A trailing perennial. Leaves oblong/ovate, mid-green. Flowers shallow funnels, lavender blue, from the leaf axils.

- Low allergen

Convolvulus tricolor 'Royal Ensign' (Convolvulaceae)

Common name: Dwarf glorybind
Height: 1ft (30cm)
Spread: 1ft (30cm)
Aspect: Full sun
Soil: Well-drained
Hardiness: Zone 8
Propagation: Seed in situ in spring
Flowering time: All summer

A bushy, short-lived perennial grown usually as an annual. Flowers solitary, open shallow funnels, deep blue with a yellow center, each lasting but one day.

- Low allergen
- Must not be moved
- Short-lived

Coreopsis grandiflora 'Early Sunrise'

Coreopsis rosea 'American Dream'

Coreopsis verticillata 'Zagreb'

Corydalis lutea

Coreopsis grandiflora 'Early Sunrise' (Asteraceae)

Common name: Tickseed
Height: 18in (45cm)
Spread: 18in (45cm)
Aspect: Sun or part shade
Soil: Well-drained, fertile
Hardiness: Zone 7
Propagation: Division in spring
Flowering time: Late spring to late summer

A short-lived perennial with solitary flowers: ray florets golden yellow, with uneven outer edges, and disc florets dark yellow. Not for the hot dry garden. Often grown as an annual, as will flower in first season.

- Attracts bees
- Good cut flower
- Attracts slugs
- Highly allergenic
- Short-lived

Coreopsis rosea 'American Dream' (Asteraceae)

Common name: Rose coreopsis
Height: 2ft (60cm)
Spread: 18in (45cm)
Aspect: Sun or part shade
Soil: Well-drained, fertile
Hardiness: Zone 4
Propagation: Seed, or division, in spring
Flowering time: Summer to early autumn

A choice clone of a North American species. Flowers solitary, single, ray florets pink, disc florets yellow.

- Attracts bees
- Attracts slugs
- Highly allergenic
- Short-lived

Coreopsis verticillata 'Zagreb' (Asteraceae)

Common name: Threadleaf coreopsis
Height: 1ft (30cm)
Spread: 1ft (30cm)
Aspect: Sun or half shade
Soil: Well-drained, fertile
Hardiness: Zone 6
Propagation: Division in spring
Flowering time: Several weeks in summer

A clone with flowers of golden yellow in loose corymbs. Has the virtue of being drought-tolerant.

- Attracts bees
- Drought-tolerant
- Attracts slugs
- Highly allergenic
- Short-lived

Corydalis lutea (Papaveraceae)

Common name: Yellow corydalis
Height: 16in (40cm)
Spread: 1ft (30cm)
Aspect: Sun or half shade
Soil: Moist, fertile, well-drained
Hardiness: Zone 6
Propagation: Seed when ripe; division, in autumn
Flowering time: Late spring to early autumn

A rhizomatous, evergreen, mound-forming perennial. Leaves fern-like, light green above, glaucous below. Flowers in racemes of up to 16, spurred, golden yellow.

- Evergreen
- Handsome foliage
- Low allergen
- Attracts slugs
- Seeds everywhere

Cosmos atrosanguineus (Asteraceae)

Common name: Chocolate cosmos
Height: 30in (75cm)
Spread: 18in (45cm)
Aspect: Full sun
Soil: Moist, well-drained, fertile
Hardiness: Zone 8
Propagation: Seed in heat, in spring
Flowering time: Midsummer to autumn

A sprawling, tuberous perennial. Leaves pinnate/bipinnate, spoon-shaped, green. Flowers solitary, single, velvety, chocolate-scented, maroon. In winter in cold areas, bring indoors or cover.

- Attracts bees
- Attracts slugs
- Good cut flower
- Handsome foliage
- Scented flowers

Cynoglossum nervosum (Boraginaceae)

Common name: Chinese hound's tongue
Height: 32in (80cm)
Spread: 2ft (60cm)
Aspect: Sun or part shade
Soil: Moist, well drained
Hardiness: Zone 5
Propagation: Seed, or division, in spring
Flowering time: Mid-spring to midsummer

A hardy, clump-forming perennial. Flowers, small, azure blue, in many-flowered cymes. Not for rich soil or heavy clay.

- Must not be moved
- Prone to mildew

Cypella herbertii (Iridaceae)

Common name: None
Height 2ft (60cm)
Spread: 4in (10cm)
Aspect: Full sun
Soil: Sharply-drained
Hardiness: Zone 9
Propagation: Seed in heat, when ripe
Flowering time: All summer

Bulbous perennial with pleated, linear leaves. Flowers have broad, mustard-colored outer tepals, and brown, purple-spotted inner ones. Tender.

- Attracts slugs

Cynoglossum nervosum

Cypella herbertii

Cyrtanthus brachyscyphus (Amaryllidaceae)

Common name: Fire lily
Height: 1ft (30cm)
Spread: 4in (10cm)
Aspect: Full sun
Soil: Well-drained, fertile, humus-rich
Hardiness: Zone 9
Propagation: Seed when ripe, in heat, or by offsets, both in spring
Flowering time: Spring to summer

A deciduous, bulbous perennial. Leaves lance-shaped, bright green. Flowers red, curved tubular, in umbels. Tender.

- Low allergen

Cosmos atrosanguineus

Cyrtanthus brachyscyphus

DAHLIA (Asteraceae)
Dahlia

A genus of only some 30 species, but 20,000 cultivars. It can be divided, for our purposes here, into two categories:

1) Tall-growing varieties suitable for borders

2) Dwarf 'bedding' varieties.

All have in common that, in warm climates, they provide color in the garden from midsummer to autumn or even later. They are also excellent for cutting. They are classified according to the size of the flower as small-, medium-, and large-flowered, and according to the form of the flower into:

Single varieties
Waterlily varieties
Collerette varieties
Anemone-flowered varieties
Pompom varieties
Ball varieties
Semi-cactus varieties
Cactus varieties
Decorative varieties
Miscellaneous varieties

They are prone to attack by slugs and snails at all stages of their life cycle, and are also prone to powdery mildew. The tubers must be lifted and stored in a dry, frost-free area over winter, and are prone to rotting during winter storage. All are tender, and Zone 10, except *Dahlia merckii*, (Zone 9).

Dahlia 'David Howard' A.G.M.

Dahlia 'Bishop of Llandaff' A.G.M.

Dahlia 'Bishop of Llandaff' A.G.M. (Asteraceae)

Common name: None
Height: 4ft (1.2m)
Spread: 18in (45cm)
Aspect: Full sun
Soil: Well-drained, humus-rich, fertile
Hardiness: Zone 10
Propagation: Division, in spring
Flowering time: Midsummer to autumn

A hybrid medium-sized, 'miscellaneous' dahlia. Leaves pinnate, black-red. Flowers peony-like, semi-double, bright red. Suitable for mixed borders.

● Attracts butterflies   ● Attracts slugs
● Good cut flower
● Handsome foliage

Dahlia 'David Howard' A.G.M. (Asteraceae)

Common name: None
Height: 4ft (1.2m)
Spread: 18in (45cm)
Aspect: Sun
Soil: Well-drained, fertile, humus-rich
Hardiness: Zone 10
Propagation: Division, in spring
Flowering time: Summer to late autumn

A miniature, decorative dahlia. Flowers fully double. Ray florets flat, blunt-ended. Color orange, with a red center.

● Attracts butterflies   ● Attracts slugs
● Good cut flower

Dahlia merckii (Asteraceae)

Common name: None
Height: 6ft (1.8m)
Spread: 3ft (90cm)
Aspect: Full sun
Soil: Well-drained, fertile, humus-rich
Hardiness: Zone 9
Propagation: Seed, or division, in spring
Flowering time: Summer to autumn

A tuberous perennial from Mexico. A sprawling, ungainly, many-branched plant with medium-sized single flowers of pale pink, with a yellow center. Can be left in the ground over winter in mild areas.

● Attracts butterflies   ● Attracts slugs
● Good cut flower

Dahlia merckii

Dahlia 'Moonfire' (Asteraceae)

Common name: None
Height: 3ft (90cm)
Spread: 18in (45cm)
Aspect: Full sun
Soil: Well-drained, fertile, humus-rich
Hardiness: Zone 10
Propagation: Division, in spring
Flowering time: Summer to late autumn

A very handsome, medium-sized, single-flowered clone. Petals yellow, with dark red basal regions, and a central yellow disc.

● Attracts butterflies   ● Attracts slugs
● Good cut flower

Dahlia 'Moonfire'

Dianthus barbatus (Caryophyllaceae)

Common name: Sweet William
Height: 28in (70cm)
Spread: 1ft (30cm)
Aspect: Full sun
Soil: Well-drained
Hardiness: Zone 4
Propagation: Seed in heat in spring
Flowering time: Late spring to early summer

A very popular, short-lived perennial, grown invariably as a biennial. Flowers in dense, flat terminal clusters, single, fragrant, petals bearded, in a wide range of colors. Deadhead to prolong season.

- Scented flowers
- Highly allergenic
- Must deadhead

Dianthus chinensis 'Carpet' series (Caryophyllaceae)

Common name: Chinese pink
Height: 28in (70cm)
Spread: 9in (23cm)
Aspect: Sun
Soil: Well-drained
Hardiness: Zone 7
Propagation: Seed in heat in spring
Flowering time: All summer if deadheaded

A short-lived perennial, grown usually as an annual or a biennial. Flowers in loose terminal cymes, single, white (or red or pink).

- Highly allergenic
- Must deadhead

Dianthus chinensis 'Strawberry Parfait' (Caryophyllaceae)

Common name: None
Height: 1ft (30cm)
Spread: 9in (23cm)
Aspect: Sun
Soil: Well-drained
Hardiness: Zone 7
Propagation: Seed in heat in spring
Flowering time: All summer if deadheaded

A short-lived perennial, grown usually as an annual or biennial. Flowers in loose terminal cymes, single, cream, with dark pink centers.

- Highly allergenic
- Must deadhead

DIASCIA (Scrophulariaceae)
Twinspur

A genus of some 50 annuals and short-lived perennials from southern Africa. They are not universally hardy but some are proving to be. They like moist soil but not waterlogged conditions. They may be erect or prostrate and some sucker freely. Their inflorescences are terminal racemes, bearing tubular flowers of pink or salmon-pink for long periods in summer. They benefit from deadheading, and should be sheared over after flowering to encourage fresh growth for another season.

Diascia 'Eclat' (Scrophulariaceae)

Common name: None
Height: 1ft (30cm)
Spread: 10in (25cm)
Aspect: Sun
Soil: Moist, well-drained, fertile
Hardiness: Zone 8
Propagation: Cuttings, in spring or summer
Flowering time: All summer

Flowers tubular, spurred, deep pink racemes.

- Attracts slugs
- Short-lived

Dianthus barbatus

Dianthus chinensis 'Carpet' series

Dianthus chinensis 'Strawberry Parfait'

Diascia 'Eclat'

Diascia 'Elizabeth'

Diascia integerrima

Diascia integerrima (Scrophulariaceae)

Common name: None
Height: 1ft (30cm)
Spread: 30in (75cm)
Aspect: Sun
Soil: Moist, well-drained, fertile
Hardiness: Zone 8
Propagation: Seed in heat when ripe;
cuttings in spring or summer
Flowering time: All summer

A creeping, suckering species from South
Africa. Flowers on upright, wiry stems,
purplish-pink, spurred, in loose racemes.

- Attracts slugs
- Invasive
- Short-lived

Diascia 'Ruby Field' A.G.M.
(Scrophulariaceae)

Common name: None
Height: 10in (25cm)
Spread: 18in (45cm)
Aspect: Sun
Soil: Moist, well-drained, fertile
Hardiness: Zone 8
Propagation: Cuttings in spring or summer
Flowering time: All summer

An old favorite, one of the best. Flowers
tubular, spurred, salmon-pink, in racemes.

- Attracts slugs
- Short-lived

Dicentra 'Pearl Drops' (Papaveraceae)

Common name: None
Height: 1ft (30cm)
Spread: 18in (45cm)
Aspect: Part shade
Soil: Moist, well-drained, fertile
Hardiness: Zone 5
Propagation: Division in spring, or after the
leaves die down
Flowering time: Mid-spring to midsummer

A quiet charmer. Ferny blue-green, glaucous
foliage. Flowers pendent, white, with a hint
of pink, in racemes. May be a bit invasive
given perfect conditions.

- Handsome foliage
- Attracts slugs
- Invasive
- Poisonous
- Skin irritant

Diascia 'Ruby Field' A.G.M.

Dicentra 'Pearl Drops'

Diascia 'Elizabeth' (Scrophulariaceae)

Common name: None
Height: 1ft (30cm)
Spread: 10in (25cm)
Aspect: Sun
Soil: Moist, well-drained, fertile
Hardiness: Zone 8
Propagation: cuttings in spring or
summer
Flowering time: All summer

A hybrid Diascia. Flowers tubular, spurred,
two-tone pink and pale pink, in racemes.

- Attracts slugs
- Short-lived

Dicentra 'Spring Morning' (Papaveraceae)

Common name: None
Height: 18in (45cm)
Spread: 18in (45cm)
Aspect: Part shade
Soil: Moist, well-drained, fertile
Hardiness: Zone 5
Propagation: Division just after the leaves
die down, or in spring
Flowering time: Late summer to autumn

A rhizomatous, hardy, hybrid perennial.
Leaves ferny. Flowers in arching racemes,
pendent, pale pink.

- Handsome foliage
- Attracts slugs
- Poisonous
- Skin irritant

Eccremocarpus scaber A.G.M.
(Bignoniaceae)

Common name: Chilean gloryflower
Height: 15ft (4.5m)
Spread: 3ft (90cm)
Aspect: Full sun
Soil: Well-drained, fertile
Hardiness: Zone 9
Propagation: Seed in heat in spring
Flowering time: Late spring to autumn

An evergreen, perennial climber. Flowers
tubular, orange, with red mouths, in
racemes. Tender.

- Evergreen
- Handsome foliage

Epilobium dodonaei (Onagraceae)

Common name: Willow herb
Height: 3ft (90cm)
Spread: 8in (20cm)
Aspect: Sun or part shade
Soil: Moist, well-drained, humus-rich
Hardiness: Zone 6
Propagation: Seed when ripe; division,
spring or autumn
Flowering time: All summer

Very invasive perennial. Flowers dark pink,
in loose terminal racemes. For wild gardens.

- Attracts slugs
- Invasive
- Prone to mildew
- Seeds everywhere

Dicentra 'Spring Morning'

Eccremocarpus scaber A.G.M.

Epilobium dodonaei

ERIGERON (Asteraceae)
Erigeron

A genus of over 200 species from North
America. They are accommodating,
easy-going plants, requiring only sun
and reasonably fertile soil. Most are
reliably hardy, drought-tolerant, and can
be grown in coastal gardens,
particularly *Erigeron glaucus*. They
attract bees and butterflies and make
good cut flowers. Almost all are long-
flowering; *Erigeron karvinskianus*
blooms from early summer to late
autumn and does not require to be
deadheaded, so one could not ask for
more from a plant. On the debit side,
they are highly allergenic plants, benefit
from regular lifting and division, and
slugs are fond of their new growth.

Erigeron aurantiacus (Asteraceae)

Common name: Daisy fleabane
Height: 1ft (30cm)
Spread: 1ft (30cm)
Aspect: Sun
Soil: Well-drained, fertile, humus-rich
Hardiness: Zone 6
Propagation: Seed or division, in spring
Flowering time: All summer

A short-lived perennial. Leaves spoon-
shaped, velvety, green. Flowers solitary,
single, bright orange, with a central
yellow boss.

- Attracts bees
- Attrracts butterflies
- Drought-tolerant
- Good cut flower
- Attracts slugs
- Divide regularly
- Highly allergenic
- Short-lived

Erigeron aurantiacus

Erigeron 'Dignity' (Asteraceae)

Common name: None
Height: 20in (50cm)
Spread: 18in (45cm)
Aspect: Sun
Soil: Well-drained, fertile, humus-rich
Hardiness: Zone 5
Propagation: Division, in spring
Flowering time: Early to midsummer

Hybrid clump-forming cultivar. Flowers solitary, ray florets violet, disc florets yellow.

- Attracts bees
- Attracts butterflies
- Drought-tolerant
- Good cut flower
- Attracts slugs
- Divide regularly
- Highly allergenic

Erigeron 'Dignity'

Erigeron 'Four Winds' (Asteraceae)

Common name: None
Height: 20in (50cm)
Spread: 18in (45cm)
Aspect: Sun
Soil: Well-drained, fertile, humus-rich
Hardiness: Zone 5
Propagation: Division, in spring
Flowering time: Early to midsummer

A free-flowering cultivar. Flowers solitary, single, of strong pink, with yellow centers.

- Attracts bees
- Attracts butterflies
- Drought-tolerant
- Good cut flower
- Attracts slugs
- Divide regularly
- Highly allergenic

Erigeron 'Four Winds'

Erigeron glaucus (Asteraceae)

Common name: Beach fleabane
Height: 1ft (30cm)
Spread: 2ft (60cm)
Aspect: Sun
Soil: Well-drained, fertile, humus-rich
Hardiness: Zone 3
Propagation: Seed or division, in spring
Flowering time: Late spring to midsummer

A species from coastal regions of California and Oregon. Leaves glaucus-green. Flowers solitary, semi-double, with ray florets of pale mauve, and yellow disc florets.

- Attracts bees
- Attracts butterflies
- Drought-tolerant
- Good cut flower
- Attracts slugs
- Highly allergenic

Erigeron karvinskianus (Asteraceae)

Common name: Bonytip fleabane
Height: 1ft (30cm)
Spread: 3ft (90cm)
Aspect: Sun
Soil: Well-drained, fertile, humus-rich
Hardiness: Zone 7
Propagation: Seed or division, in spring
Flowering time: Midsummer to late autumn

As long-flowering plants go, this is in the top flight. Flowers single, small, white, becoming pink with age. Does not require deadheading. Superb wall plant. Long-lived.

- Attracts bees
- Drought-tolerant
- Highly allergenic
- Seeds everywhere

Erigeron glaucus

Erigeron karvinskianus

Erigeron 'Quakeress'

Erigeron 'Serenity'

Eriophyllum lanatum

Erigeron 'Quakeress' (Asteraceae)

Common name: None
Height: 2ft (60cm)
Spread: 18in (45cm)
Aspect: Sun
Soil: Well-drained, fertile, humus-rich
Hardiness: Zone 5
Propagation: Division, in spring
Flowering time: Early to midsummer

A clump-forming perennial. Leaves gray-green. Flowers single, white, with a hint of pink, and yellow centers, in corymbs.

- Attracts bees
- Attracts butterflies
- Drought tolerant
- Good cut flower
- Attracts slugs
- Divide regularly
- Highly allergenic

Erigeron 'Serenity' (Asteraceae)

Common name: None
Height: 30in (75cm)
Spread: 18in (45cm)
Aspect: Sun
Soil: Well-drained, fertile, humus-rich
Hardiness: Zone 5
Propagation: Division, in spring
Flowering time: Early to midsummer

A lax cultivar. Flowers semi-double, violet-mauve, with yellow centers, in corymbs.

- Attracts bees
- Attracts butterflies
- Drought-tolerant
- Good cut flower
- Attracts slugs
- Divide regularly
- Highly allergenic

Eriophyllum lanatum (Asteraceae)

Common name: Wooly eriophyllum
Height: 2ft (60cm)
Spread: 2ft (60cm)
Aspect: Sun
Soil: Sharply-drained
Hardiness: Zone 5
Propagation: Seed in autumn; division in spring
Flowering time: Late spring to summer

A hardy, mildly invasive perennial. Leaves silvery-gray, white-wooly. Flowers yellow daisies, with dark yellow centers, singly or in corymbs.

- Drought-tolerant
- Handsome foliage
- Attracts slugs
- Highly allergenic
- Invasive

ERODIUM (Geraniaceae)
Erodium

A genus of some 60 species of perennials, annuals, and subshrubs, with handsome foliage and a long flowering period. They are mostly hardy, but not universally so, and are drought-tolerant. The flowers have a close resemblance to those of the *Geranium*, but have five stamens as opposed to the ten in *Geranium*. They are good coastal plants, like sun, good drainage, and will self-seed unless deadheaded.

Erodium 'Fran's choice'

Erodium 'Fran's choice' (Geraniaceae)

Common name: None
Height: 8in (20cm)
Spread: 8in (20cm)
Aspect: Sun
Soil: Sharply-drained
Hardiness: Zone 7
Propagation: Division, in spring
Flowering time: Early summer to autumn

A hybrid clone with pinnatisect, mid-green leaves. Flowers pink, in short terminal umbels.

- Drought-tolerant
- Low allergen
- Seeds everywhere

Erodium manescaui

Erodium 'Merstham Pink'

Erysimum linifolium 'Variegatum'

Erodium manescaui (Geraniaceae)

Common name: Pyrenees heronbill
Height: 18in (45cm)
Spread: 8in (20cm)
Aspect: Sun
Soil: Sharply-drained, humus-rich
Hardiness: Zone 6
Propagation: Seed when ripe; division, in spring
Flowering time: Early summer to autumn

A handsome species. Leaves pinnate, toothed, hairy, mid-green. Flowers in long-stemmed umbels, magenta-colored, the upper pair of petals spotted.

- Drought-tolerant
- Low allergen
- Seeds everywhere

Erodium 'Merstham Pink' (Geraniaceae)

Common name: None
Height: 9in (23cm)
Spread: 10in (25cm)
Aspect: Sun
Soil: Sharply-drained
Hardiness: Zone 6
Propagation: Division, in spring
Flowering time: Early summer to autumn

A hybrid clone, with ferny, carrot-like foliage of dark green. Flowers in umbels, pink. Not spectacular, but very reliable. Good wall plant. Does not self-seed.

- Drought-tolerant
- Handsome foliage
- Low allergen

Erysimum linifolium 'Variegatum' (Brassicaceae)

Common name: Alpine wallflower
Height: 28in (70cm)
Spread: 10in (25cm)
Aspect: Sun
Soil: Well-drained, humus-rich
Hardiness: Zone 6
Propagation: Softwood cuttings, with a heel, in spring or summer
Flowering time: Mid-spring to early autumn

A woody, short-lived, evergreen perennial with linear leaves of pale green, edged in cream. Flowers lilac, in racemes.

- Drought-tolerant
- Evergreen
- Handsome foliage
- Attracts slugs
- Prone to mildew
- Short-lived

Eucomis autumnalis (Hyacinthaceae)

Common name: Pineapple flower/lily
Height: 1ft (30cm)
Spread: 8in (20cm)
Aspect: Sun
Soil: Well-drained, fertile, dry in winter
Hardiness: Zone 8
Propagation: Offsets in spring
Flowering time: Late summer to late autumn

A half-hardy bulbous perennial. Leaves wavy-margined, pale green. Flowers pale greenish-white, in dense racemes.

- Drought-tolerant
- Good cut flower
- Handsome foliage
- Attracts slugs

Eucomis autumnalis

Eucomis bicolor (Hyacinthaceae)

Common name: Pineapple flower/lily
Height: 2ft (60cm)
Spread: 10in (25cm)
Aspect: Sun
Soil: Well-drained, fertile, dry in winter
Hardiness: Zone 8
Propagation: Offsets in spring
Flowering time: Midsummer to late autumn

A half-hardy, bulbous perennial. Leaves wavy-edged, bright green. Flowers pale green, with purple-edged tepals, in dense racemes, topped by pineapple-like bracts.

- Drought-tolerant
- Good cut flower
- Handsome foliage
- Attracts slugs

Fragaria 'Lipstick' (Rosaceae)

Common name: Strawberry
Height: 6in (15cm)
Spread: Indefinite
Aspect: Sun or part shade
Soil: Moist, well-drained, fertile
Hardiness: Zone 5
Propagation: Plantlets, from runners, at any time
Flowering time: Late spring to mid-autumn

A selected, sterile clone of the well-known stoloniferous fruiting perennial. Evergreen in mild areas. Flowers single, cerise, in cymes. *Fragaria* 'Pink Panda' has pink flowers.

- Handsome foliage
- Invasive
- Prone to mildew

Gaillardia x *grandiflora* 'Burgunder' (Asteraceae)

Common name: None
Height: 2ft (60cm)
Spread: 18in (45cm)
Aspect: Sun
Soil: Sharply-drained, poor
Hardiness: Zone 4
Propagation: Softwood cuttings, in spring
Flowering time: Early summer to autumn

A shortlived clone of garden origin. Flowers large single daisies, with deep wine-red ray florets, and yellow-brown disc florets. Cut back hard in late summer to improve chance of over-wintering

- Drought-tolerant
- Good cut flower
- Attracts slugs
- Highly allergenic
- Prone to mildew
- Requires staking
- Short-lived

Gaillardia x *grandiflora* 'Kobold' (Asteraceae)

Common name: None
Height: 1ft (30cm)
Spread: 18in (45cm)
Aspect: Sun
Soil: Sharply-drained, poor
Hardiness: Zone 4
Propagation: Softwood cuttings in spring
Flowering time: Mid-summer to autumn

A very compact, dwarf, short-lived hybrid clone. Flowers single, ray florets red, tipped yellow, disc florets deep red-brown. Cut back hard in late summer to improve chance of over-wintering.

- Drought-tolerant
- Good cut flower
- Attracts slugs
- Highly allergenic
- Prone to mildew
- Short-lived

Eucomis bicolor

Fragaria 'Lipstick'

Gaillardia x *grandiflora* 'Burgunder'

Gaillardia x *grandiflora* 'Kobold'

Gaillardia x *grandiflora* 'Red Plume' (PBR) (Asteraceae)

Common name: None
Height: 18in (45cm)
Spread: 18in (45cm)
Aspect: Sun
Soil: Sharply-drained, poor
Hardiness: Zone 4
Propagation: Softwood cuttings in spring
Flowering time: Mid-summer to autumn

A very recently introduced variety. Flowers have ray florets of deep rich red, and disc florets of brown-red. Cut back hard in late summer to improve chance of over-wintering.

- Attracts slugs
- Drought-tolerant
- Good cut flower
- Highly allergenic
- Prone to mildew

Galega x *hartlandii* 'Alba' A.G.M. (Papilionaceae)

Common name: Goats-rue
Height: 5ft (1.5m)
Spread: 3ft (90cm)
Aspect: Sun or part shade
Soil: Moist
Hardiness: Zone 4
Propagation: Seed or division, in spring
Flowering time: Early summer to autumn

A tall, mildly invasive perennial. Flowers in erect, axillary racemes, pea-like, white. Dead-head to prevent self-seeding.

- Good cut flower
- Invasive
- Must not be moved
- Requires staking
- Seeds everywhere

Galega 'Lady Wilson' (Papilionaceae)

Common name: None
Height: 5ft (1.5m)
Spread: 3ft (90cm)
Aspect: Sun or half shade
Soil: Moist
Hardiness: Zone 4
Propagation: Seed or division, in spring
Flowering time: Early summer to autumn

A tall, mildly invasive perennial. Flowers in racemes, bicolored, mauve-pink and white. Deadhead to prevent self-seeding.

- Good cut flower
- Invasive
- Must not be moved
- Requires staking
- Seeds everywhere

Galega officinalis (Papilionaceae)

Common name: Common goats-rue
Height: 5ft (1.5m)
Spread: 3ft (90cm)
Aspect: Sun or part shade
Soil: Moist
Hardiness: Zone 4
Propagation: Seed, or division, in spring
Flowering time: Early summer to autumn

A tall, vigorous perennial. Flowers white, mauve or (as here) bicolored, in racemes. Deadhead to prevent self-seeding.

- Good cut flower
- Invasive
- Must not be moved
- Requires staking
- Seeds everywhere

Gaillardia x *grandiflora* 'Red Plume' (PBR)

Galega x *hartlandii* 'Alba' A.G.M.

Galega 'Lady Wilson'

Galega officinalis

Galium odoratum (Rubiaceae)

Common name: None
Height: 18in (45cm)
Spread: Indefinite
Aspect: Sun or part shade
Soil: Moist, humus-rich
Hardiness: Zone 3
Propagation: Seed when ripe; division, spring/autumn
Flowering time: Late spring to midsummer

A rhizomatous perennial useful for ground-cover. Flowers white, star-shaped, scented, in umbel-like cymes.

- Scented flowers   - Invasive

Galium odoratum

Gaura lindheimeri A.G.M. (Onagraceae)

Common name: White gaura
Height: 5ft (1.5m)
Spread: 3ft (90cm)
Aspect: Sun
Soil: Sharply-drained
Hardiness: Zone 4
Propagation: Seed, or division, in spring
Flowering time: Late spring to autumn

A hardy, short-lived perennial from Texas. Flowers white, fading to pink, in loose panicles.

- Drought-tolerant   - Requires staking
                       - Short-lived

Gaura lindheimeri A.G.M.

Gaura lindheimeri 'Siskyou Pink' (Onagraceae)

Common name: None
Height: 5ft (1.5m)
Spread: 3ft (90cm)
Aspect: Sun
Soil: Sharply-drained,
Hardiness: Zone 4
Propagation: Division, in spring
Flowering time: Late spring to early autumn

A charming clone, with flowers of pale to deep pink, in panicles.

- Drought-tolerant   - Requires staking
                       - Short-lived

Gazania 'Christopher Lloyd' (Asteraceae)

Common name: Treasure flower
Height: 8in (20cm)
Spread: 8in (20cm)
Aspect: Full sun
Soil: Sharply-drained
Hardiness: Zone 9
Propagation: Basal cuttings in late summer, or early autumn
Flowering time: All summer, open only in sun

A selected clone of a tender, evergreen perennial. Leaves shiny-green above, white-hairy below. Flowers solitary, single, pink ray florets with a dark purple base, and a yellow center.

- Drought-tolerant   - Highly allergenic
- Evergreen   - Must deadhead
- Good cut flower

Gaura lindheimeri 'Siskyou Pink'

Gazania 'Christopher Lloyd'

Gazania 'Daybreak' series A.G.M.

Gazania 'Daybreak' series A.G.M.
(Asteraceae)

Common name: None
Height: 8in (20cm)
Spread: 8in (20cm)
Aspect: Full sun
Soil: Sharply-drained
Hardiness: Zone 9
Propagation: Seed in heat in spring
Flowering time: All summer

A tender evergreen perennial from S. Africa.
Leaves glossy-green above, silky-white hairy
below. Flowers solitary, single, opening only
in sun; white, orange, yellow or pink.

- Drought-tolerant
- Evergreen
- Good cut flower
- Highly allergenic
- Must deadhead

GERANIUM (Geraniaceae)
Cranesbill

A genus of 300 species, and
innumerable hybrids. They are usually
long-flowering, long-lived, easy to grow,
and have handsome foliage; as a result
they are indispensable. They come from
a widely diverse group of habitats in the
wild, and so their cultural requirements
vary; for the same reason, their degree
of hardiness can vary widely. What they
all have in common is a dislike of boggy
or waterlogged conditions.

The flowers are flat or saucer-shaped,
and may be in cymes, umbels, or
panicles. Most species are rather floppy
and some type of support is usually
necessary; all should be sheared over
after flowering to encourage next year's
growth. All are drought-tolerant and
low allergen. *Geranium thunbergii* self-
seeds to a totally unacceptable degree,
so should be avoided at all costs, or
deadheaded.

About 25 have been given the
accolade of an Award of Garden Merit
by the Royal Horticultural Society.

Geranium 'Ann Folkard' A.G.M.
(Geraniaceae)

Common name: None
Height: 2ft (60cm)
Spread 5ft (1.5m)
Aspect: Sun or part shade
Soil: Well-drained
Hardiness: Zone 7
Propagation: Division, in spring
Flowering time: Midsummer to mid-autumn

A very handsome scrambling ground-
covering cultivar. Leaves yellow at first,
becoming green. Flowers rich magenta with
dark centers.

- Drought-tolerant
- Handsome foliage
- Low allergen
- Attracts slugs
- Prone to mildew
- Requires space

Geranium himalayense 'Plenum'

Geranium himalayense 'Plenum'
(Geraniaceae)

Common name: None
Height: 10in (25cm)
Spread: 18in (45cm)
Aspect: Any
Soil: Well-drained
Hardiness: Zone 4
Propagation: Seed, or division, in spring
Flowering time: Early summer: intermittent

A double form which is more compact than
the single form. Flowers fully double,
purplish-pink, with dark veins.

- Drought-tolerant
- Handsome foliage
- Low allergen
- Attracts slugs
- Prone to mildew

Geranium maderense A.G.M. (Geraniaceae)

Common name: None
Height: 5ft (1.5m)
Spread: 5ft (1.5m)
Aspect: Sun
Soil: Well-drained
Hardiness: Zone 9
Propagation: Seed or division, in spring
Flowering time: Late spring to midsummer

A tender perennial from Madeira. Leaves
lobed, toothed, bright green. Flowers flat,
magenta, with pale veins, in panicles.

- Drought-tolerant
- Handsome foliage
- Low allergen
- Attracts slugs
- Prone to mildew

Geranium 'Ann Folkard' A.G.M.

Geranium maderense A.G.M.

Geranium psilostemon A.G.M.

Geranium riversleianum 'Mavis Simpson'

Geranium psilostemon A.G.M.
(Geraniaceae)

Common name: None
Height: 4ft (1.2m)
Spread: 4ft (1.2m)
Aspect: Sun or part shade
Soil: Well-drained
Hardiness: Zone 6
Propagation: Seed or division, in spring
Flowering time: Early to late summer

A hardy perennial from Armenia. Leaves
lobed, red in spring and autumn, green in
summer. Flowers large, deep magenta, in
upright cymes. Excellent species.

- Drought-tolerant
- Handsome foliage
- Low allergen
- Attracts slugs
- Prone to mildew

Geranium riversleianum 'Mavis Simpson'
(Geraniaceae)

Common name: None
Height: 2ft (60cm)
Spread: 3ft (90cm)
Aspect: Sun or part shade
Soil: Well-drained
Hardiness: Zone 7
Propagation: Division, in spring
Flowering time: All summer

A hybrid with flowers of pink, with pale
pink centers, in loose cymes. Very desirable.

- Drought-tolerant
- Handsome foliage
- Low allergen
- Attracts slugs
- Prone to mildew

**Geranium riversleianum 'Russell Pritchard'
A.G.M.** (Geraniaceae)

Common name: None
Height: 1ft (30cm)
Spread: 3ft (90cm)
Aspect: Sun or part shade
Soil: Well-drained
Hardiness: Zone 7
Propagation: Division, in spring
Flowering time: All summer

A very free-flowering clone. Flowers small,
deep magenta, in loose cymes.

- Drought-tolerant
- Handsome foliage
- Low allergen
- Attracts slugs
- Prone to mildew

Geranium riversleianum 'Russell Pritchard' A.G.M.

**Geranium wallichianum 'Buxton's variety'
A.G.M.** (Geraniaceae)

Common name: None
Height: 1ft (30cm)
Spread: 3ft (90cm)
Aspect: Sun or part shade
Soil: Well-drained
Hardiness: Zone 7
Propagation: Seed or division, in spring
Flowering time: Midsummer to mid-autumn

A trailing hardy perennial. Flowers sky blue
with large, white, veined centers, in loose
cymes. Can come true from seed.

- Drought-tolerant
- Handsome foliage
- Low allergen
- Attracts slugs
- Prone to mildew

Geranium wallichianum 'Buxton's variety'

Gerbera jamesonii 'Pandora' series

Geum 'Lady Stratheden' A.G.M.

Gerbera jamesonii 'Pandora' series (Asteraceae)

Common name: Transvaal daisy
Height: 16in (40cm)
Spread: 18in (45cm)
Aspect: Full sun
Soil: Well-drained, fertile
Hardiness: Zone 8
Propagation: Seed in heat, or division, in spring
Flowering time: Late spring to late summer

A strain raised from seed; the cultivars have a basal rosette of leaves, and single or double flowers of red, yellow, orange, or pink.

- Good cut flower
- Handsome foliage
- Attracts slugs
- Must not be moved
- Prone to mildew

Geum 'Lady Stratheden' A.G.M. (Rosaceae)

Common name: None
Height: 2ft (60cm)
Spread: 2ft (60cm)
Aspect: Sun or part shade
Soil: Well-drained, fertile
Hardiness: Zone 6
Propagation: Division in spring or autumn
Flowering time: All summer

A hybrid of *Geum chiloense*. Leaves pinnate, hairy, green. Flowers semi-double, yellow, in cymes of up to 5. Will flower well only if lifted and divided every other year.

- Handsome foliage
- Low allergen
- Divide regularly

Geum 'Mrs J. Bradshaw' (Rosaceae)

Common name: None
Height: 2ft (60cm)
Spread: 2ft (60cm)
Aspect: Sun or part shade
Soil: Well-drained, fertile
Hardiness: Zone 6
Propagation: Division in spring or autumn
Flowering time: Early to late summer

A *Geum chiloense* hybrid. Leaves pinnate, hairy green. Flowers semi-double, red, in cymes of up to 5. Will flower well only if lifted and divided every other year

- Handsome foliage
- Low allergen
- Divide regularly

Geum 'Mrs J. Bradshaw'

Gillenia trifoliata A.G.M. (Rosaceae)

Common name: Bowman's-root
Height: 3ft (90cm)
Spread: 2ft (60cm)
Aspect: Part shade
Soil: Acid, moist, well-drained
Hardiness: Zone 4
Propagation: Seed or division, in spring or autumn
Flowering time: Late spring to late summer

A rhizomatous, perennial woodlander. Leaves bronze-green, veined. Flowers asymmetric, white, starry.

- Good cut flower
- Attracts slugs
- Requires staking

Gillenia trifoliata A.G.M.

43

Gloriosa superba A.G.M.

Gypsophila paniculata 'Rosenschleier'

Gypsophila repens 'Dorothy Teacher' A.G.M.

Haplopappus glutinosus

Gloriosa superba A.G.M. (Colchicaceae)

Common name: None
Height: 6ft (1.8m)
Spread: 1ft (30cm)
Aspect: Full sun
Soil: Well-drained, fertile
Hardiness: Zone 9
Propagation: Seed in heat, or separation of tubers, in spring
Flowering time: Summer to autumn

A tuberous, climbing perennial. Flowers nodding, petals reflexed, wavy-edged, red or purple, yellow-margined, or pure yellow, with long protruding stamens. Tender.

- Poisonous
- Skin-irritant

Gypsophila paniculata 'Rosenschleier' A.G.M. (Caryophyllaceae)

Common name: None
Height: 2ft (60cm)
Spread: 3ft (90cm)
Aspect: Full sun
Soil: Sharply-drained
Hardiness: Zone 4
Propagation: root cuttings, or grafting, in late winter
Flowering time: Mid and late summer

A bushy, dense perennial. Leaves blue-green. Flowers in many-flowered panicles, double, white becoming pink.

- Attracts bees
- Drought-tolerant
- Good cut flower
- Handsome foliage
- Must not be moved
- Short-lived

Gypsophila repens 'Dorothy Teacher' A.G.M. (Caryophyllaceae)

Common name: Creeping gypsophila
Height: 2in (5cm)
Spread: 16in (40cm)
Aspect: Full sun
Soil: Sharply-drained
Hardiness: Zone 4
Propagation: Root cuttings or grafting, in late winter
Flowering time: Long periods in summer

A mat-forming perennial. Leaves blue-green. Flowers star-shaped, pale pink, in loose corymb-like panicles.

- Attracts bees
- Drought-tolerant
- Handsome foliage
- Must not be moved
- Short-lived

Haplopappus glutinosus (Asteraceae)

Common name: None
Height: 6in (15cm)
Spread: 1ft (30cm)
Aspect: Full sun
Soil: Sharply-drained
Hardiness: Zone 9
Propagation: Seed when ripe, or in spring
Flowering time: Long periods in summer

A tender, cushion-forming, evergreen perennial. Leaves sticky, dark green. Flowers solitary, single yellow. Must be deadheaded.

- Drought-tolerant
- Evergreen
- Good cut flower
- Must deadhead

Hedysarum coronarium

Helenium 'Pumilum magnificum'

Helenium 'Rubinzwerg'

Helianthus 'Lemon Queen'

Hedysarum coronarium (Papilionaceae)

Common name: Sulla sweetvetch
Height: 3ft (90cm)
Spread: 2ft (60cm)
Aspect: Sun
Soil: Sharply-drained
Hardiness: Zone 3
Propagation: Seed when ripe, or in spring
Flowering time: Throughout spring

A short-lived perennial. Flowers pea-like, scented, deep red, in racemes, on erect stems.

- Good cut flower
- Scented flowers
- Must not be moved
- Short-lived

Helenium 'Pumilum magnificum' (Asteraceae)

Common name: None
Height: 3ft (90cm)
Spread: 2ft (60cm)
Aspect: Sun
Soil: Moist, well-drained, humus-rich
Hardiness: Zone 5
Propagation: Division, spring or autumn
Flowering time: Late summer to mid-autumn

An erect, hardy perennial. Flowers solitary, single, daisy-like, ray florets yellow, disc florets brown. Needs to be deadheaded.

- Attracts bees
- Good cut flower
- Divide regularly
- Highly allergenic
- Must deadhead
- Poisonous
- Requires staking
- Skin irritant

Helenium 'Rubinzwerg' (Asteraceae)

Common name: None
Height: 3ft (90cm)
Spread: 18in (45cm)
Aspect: Sun
Soil: Moist, well-drained, humus-rich
Hardiness: Zone 5
Propagation: Division, spring or autumn
Flowering time: Late summer to late autumn

A recent introduction of great promise. Flowers solitary, single, ray florets dark red, discs yellow. Deadheading prolongs flowering.

- Attracts bees
- Good cut flower
- Divide regularly
- Highly allergenic
- Poisonous
- Skin irritant

Helianthus 'Lemon Queen' (Asteraceae)

Common name: None
Height: 6ft (1.8m)
Spread: 4ft (1.2m)
Aspect: Sun
Soil: Moist, well-drained, humus-rich
Hardiness: Zone 5
Propagation: Division, spring or autumn
Flowering time: Late summer to mid-autumn

A very tall, free-flowering, rhizomatous, invasive, hardy perennial. Flowers single, pale yellow, with dark yellow centers.

- Attracts bees
- Good cut flower
- Highly allergenic
- Invasive
- Prone to mildew
- Requires staking
- Skin irritant

Hemerocallis 'Chicago Royal Robe'

Hemerocallis 'Corky' A.G.M.

HEMEROCALLIS *(Hemerocallidaceae)*
Day-lily

A genus of only some 15 species, but some 30,000 hybrids are in cultivation. Of the species, *HH. fulva* and *lilio-asphodelus* are highly invasive weeds.

Day-lilies are clump-forming, and do best if lifted and divided every few years. They thrive in sun or light shade, and are not demanding as to soil, as long as it does not dry out. They may be evergreen, or semi-evergreen. Flowering time is summer; each flower lasts for only about 12 hours, or 16 hours in the instance of extended-flowering cultivars (some are night-flowering) but is followed by others in succession over many weeks. Some cultivars are scented. All are low-allergen and suitable for allergic gardeners. They make excellent cut flowers, and are beloved of the flower-arranger. The flower is composed of three petals and three sepals, which alternate, giving, in general, a star shape, and which are known collectively as tepals.

Hemerocallis 'Chicago Royal Robe' (Hemerocallidaceae)

Common name: Day-lily
Height: 2ft (60cm)
Spread: 1ft (30cm)
Aspect: Sun
Soil: Moist, well-drained, humus-rich
Hardiness: Zone 5
Propagation: Division, in spring or autumn
Flowering time: Several weeks in midsummer

A hardy, semi-evergreen Day-lily. Flowers large, purplish-pink, with a yellow throat.

- Attracts bees
- Good cut flower
- Low allergen
- Attracts slugs
- Divide regularly

Hemerocallis 'Corky' A.G.M. (Hemerocallidaceae)

Common name: Day-lily
Height: 3ft (90cm)
Spread: 2ft (60cm)
Aspect: Sun
Soil: Moist, well-drained, humus-rich
Hardiness: Zone 5
Propagation: Division, in spring or autumn
Flowering time: All summer

A very free-flowering, evergreen perennial, with black stems which provide a good contrast for the small, lemon-yellow flowers, borne profusely. One of the best Day-lilies.

- Attracts bees
- Evergreen
- Good cut flower
- Low allergen
- Attracts slugs
- Divide regularly

Hemerocallis 'Frans Hals' (Hemerocallidaceae)

Common name: Day-lily
Height: 2ft (60cm)
Spread: 2ft (60cm)
Aspect: Sun
Soil: Moist, well-drained, humus-rich
Hardiness: Zone 5
Propagation: Division, in spring or autumn
Flowering time: All summer

A hardy perennial bicolored Day-lily. Flowers have rust petals and creamy sepals.

- Attracts bees
- Good cut flower
- Low allergen
- Attracts slugs
- Divide regularly

Hemerocallis 'Green Flutter' A.G.M. (Hemerocallidaceae)

Common name: Day-lily
Height: 20in (50cm)
Spread: 3ft (90cm)
Aspect: Sun
Soil: Moist, well-drained, humus-rich
Hardiness: Zone 5
Propagation: Division, in spring or autumn
Flowering time: All summer

An extended-blooming, evergreen, nocturnal-flowering Day-lily. Flowers star-shaped, with yellow petals, yellow sepals with ruffled margins, and a hint of green in the throat.

- Evergreen
- Good cut flower
- Low allergen
- Attracts slugs
- Divide regularly

Hemerocallis 'Frans Hals'

Hemerocallis 'Green Flutter' A.G.M.

Hemerocallis 'Silver Veil'
(Hemerocallidaceae)

Common name: Day-lily
Height 2ft (60cm)
Spread: 3ft (90cm)
Aspect: Sun
Soil: Moist, well-drained, humus-rich
Hardiness: Zone 5
Propagation: Division, in spring or autumn
Flowering time: All summer

A handsome, semi-evergreen, bicolored Day-lily. Flowers have brown-red petals, flesh pink sepals, and a yellow throat.

- Good cut flower
- Low allergen
- Attracts slugs
- Divide regularly

Hemerocallis 'Stafford'
(Hemerocallidaceae)

Common name: Day-lily
Height: 28in (70cm)
Spread: 3ft (90cm)
Aspect: Sun
Soil: Moist, well-drained, humus-rich
Hardiness: Zone 5
Propagation: Division, in spring or autumn
Flowering time: Several weeks in midsummer

A free-flowering, evergreen perennial. Flowers deep scarlet, with yellow midribs and throat.

- Good cut flower
- Low allergen
- Attracts slugs
- Divide regularly

Hemerocallis 'Tutunkhamun'
(Hemerocallidaceae)

Common name: Day-lily
Height: 2ft (60cm)
Spread: 3ft (90cm)
Aspect: Sun
Soil: Moist, well-drained, humus-rich
Hardiness: Zone 5
Propagation: Division, in spring or autumn
Flowering time: Several weeks in midsummer

A semi-evergreen, hybrid Day lily. Flowers have brown petals with a central cream stripe, yellow sepals, and a yellow throat.

- Good cut flower
- Low allergen
- Attracts slugs
- Divide regularly

Heuchera 'Red Spangles' A.G.M.
(Saxifragaceae)

Common name: None
Height: 20in (50cm)
Spread: 10in (25cm)
Aspect: Any
Soil: Moist, well-drained, fertile
Hardiness: Zone 4
Propagation: Division, in autumn
Flowering time: All summer

Handsome, evergreen, marbled leaves. Flowers in open panicles, red. Good ground cover.

- Evergreen
- Good cut flower
- Handsome foliage
- Low allergen
- Divide regularly

Hemerocallis 'Silver Veil'

Hemerocallis 'Stafford'

Hemerocallis 'Tutunkhamun'

Heuchera 'Red Spangles' A.G.M.

47

x *Heucherella alba* 'Bridget Bloom' (Saxifragaceae)

Common name: None
Height: 16in (40cm)
Spread: 1ft (30cm)
Aspect: Any
Soil: Acid to neutral, moist, well-drained
Hardiness: Zone 5
Propagation: Division, in autumn or spring
Flowering time: Late spring to mid-autumn

An intergeneric hybrid between *Heuchera* and *Tiarella*. Leaves evergreen, toothed, mid-green. Flowers small, pink, in panicles. Good ground cover, even in shade.

- Evergreen
- Good cut flower
- Low allergen

Hylomecon japonica (Papaveraceae)

Common name: None
Height: 8in (20cm)
Spread: 18in (45cm)
Aspect: Part or full shade
Soil: Acid, moist, humus-rich
Hardiness: Zone 7
Propagation: Seed when ripe; division, in spring
Flowering time: Late spring to summer

A rhizomatous woodlander. Handsome leaves. Flowers solitary single, saucer-shaped, 4-petaled, dark yellow.

- Handsome foliage
- Attracts slugs
- Invasive

Hypericum cerastioides (Clusiaceae)

Common name: Rhodope St-John's-wort
Height: 8in (20cm)
Spread: 18in (45cm)
Aspect: Sun
Soil: Sharply-drained
Hardiness: Zone 7
Propagation: Division, in spring or autumn
Flowering time: Late spring to early summer

A herb from the Near East. Leaves downy, gray-green. Flowers in cymes of up to 5, star-shaped, yellow. Prune by deadheading and removing wayward shoots after flowering.

- Drought-tolerant
- Evergreen
- Handsome foliage
- Low allergen

Hylomecon japonica

Hypericum cerastioides

IMPATIENS (*Balsaminaceae*)
Impatiens

A genus of more than 800 species from a wide variety of habitats, many of these being moist in tropical and sub-tropical regions; the majority of species are therefore tender. They have succulent brittle stems and fleshy leaves, and so are not wind-tolerant. The 5-petaled flowers may be solitary, in racemes or clusters, and the seed capsules are explosive; this is important with some species, which can become highly invasive. They grow in sun or in shade in the wild. Some species have handsome foliage.

They make excellent long-flowering bedding plants, and do not require to be deadheaded; they thrive in moist, well-drained humus-rich soil, in part shade. Seedlings are very prone to damping-off, and planting out should be delayed until all danger of frost has passed.

Impatiens 'New Guinea' hybrids (Balsaminaceae)

Common name: None
Height: 1ft (30cm)
Spread: 9in (23cm)
Aspect: Sun or part shade
Soil: Moist, well-drained, fertile
Hardiness: Zone 10
Propagation: Seed in heat in early spring
Flowering time: All summer

A race of perennials from crosses between several species. Foliage bronzed, handsome, often variegated. Flowers in many shades, or bicolored. Usually grown as annuals.

- Low allergen
- Seeds everywhere

x *Heucherella alba* 'Bridget Bloom'

Impatiens 'New Guinea' hybrids

Impatiens niamniamensis 'Congo Cockatoo'

Impatiens niamniamensis 'Congo Cockatoo' (Balsamaceae)

Common name: None
Height: 3ft (90cm)
Spread: 15in (38cm)
Aspect: Sun or part shade
Soil: Moist, well-drained, humus-rich
Hardiness: Zone 10
Propagation: Softwood cuttings in spring or early summer
Flowering time: All year on and off

A short-lived perennial. Flowers hooded, narrow, yellow and red, with hooked spurs.

● Low allergen   ● Short-lived

Impatiens walleriana 'Accent' series A.G.M. (Balsaminaceae)

Common name: Sultan snapweed
Height: 2ft (60cm)
Spread: 2ft (60cm)
Aspect: Sun or part shade
Soil: Moist, well-drained, humus-rich
Hardiness: Zone 10
Propagation: Seed in heat in spring
Flowering time: All summer

A tender perennial grown almost universally as an annual. Flowers flat, in many shades, or bicolored. Does not require to be deadheaded. Deservedly highly popular.

● Low allergen

Ipomoea lobata (Convolvulaceae)

Common name: None
Height: 15ft (4.5m)
Spread: 3ft (90cm)
Aspect: Full sun
Soil: Well-drained, fertile
Hardiness: Zone 8
Propagation: Seed in heat in spring
Flowering time: Summer to autumn

A perennial climber, grown usually as an annual. Stems crimson-flushed. Flowers in dense, one-sided racemes, tubular, scarlet, becoming orange/yellow with age.

● Prone to mildew

Impatiens walleriana 'Accent' series A.G.M.

Ipomoea lobata

Lapageria rosea A.G.M. (Liliaceae)

Common name: Red Chile-bells
Height: 15ft (4.5m)
Spread: 3ft (90cm)
Aspect: Part shade
Soil: Acid, moist, well-drained, dry in winter
Hardiness: Zone 9
Propagation: Soaked seed in heat in spring
Flowering time: Summer to late autumn

A climbing, twining, evergreen perennial. Flowers long trumpets, single or in two and threes, pink or red. No pruning needed.

● Evergreen   ● Requires space

Lapageria rosea A.G.M.

49

Laurentia axillaris 'Blue Stars'

Limonium sinuatum

Linaria purpurea

Linaria purpurea 'Winifred's Delight'

Laurentia axillaris 'Blue Stars' (Campanulaceae)

Common name: None
Height: 1ft (30cm)
Spread: 1ft (30cm)
Aspect: Full sun
Soil: Well-drained, fertile
Hardiness: Zone 9
Propagation: Seed in heat in spring; softwood cuttings in summer
Flowering time: Spring to autumn

A tender perennial, grown usually as an annual. Flowers small, star-shaped, solitary, long-tubed, dark blue, abundant. Good in baskets and as a bedding plant.

- Skin irritant

Limonium sinuatum (Plumbaginaceae)

Common name: Notch-leaf sea-lavender
Height: 16in (40cm)
Spread: 2ft (60cm)
Aspect: Sun
Soil: Sharply-drained
Hardiness: Zone 9
Propagation: Seed, or division, in spring
Flowering time: Early to late summer

A tender perennial usually grown as an annual in cold areas. Flowers on stiff stems, in panicles, in many colors, tiny funnel-shaped, enclosed in differently-colored calyces.

- Can be dried
- Prone to mildew
- Drought-resistant
- Good cut flower

Linaria purpurea (Scrophulariaceae)

Common name: Purple toadflax
Height: 3ft (90cm)
Spread: 1ft (30cm)
Aspect: Sun
Soil: Sharply-drained
Hardiness: Zone 6
Propagation: Seed, or division, in spring
Flowering time: Early summer to autumn

An erect, hardy perennial. Flowers two-lipped, snapdragon-like, pink, purple or violet, with curved spurs, in dense, slender racemes.

- Drought-tolerant
- Prone to mildew
- Good cut flower
- Seeds everywhere

Linaria purpurea 'Winifred's Delight' (Scrophulariaceae)

Common name: None
Height: 1ft (30cm)
Spread: 1ft (30cm)
Aspect: Sun
Soil: Sharply-drained
Hardiness: Zone 6
Propagation: Seed, or division, in spring
Flowering time: Early summer to autumn

A hardy perennial. Flowers in slender, dense racemes, snapdragon-like, with curved spurs, creamy-yellow.

- Drought-tolerant
- Prone to mildew
- Good cut flower
- Seeds everywhere

Linum Gemmell's hybrid A.G.M. (Linaceae)

Common name: None
Height: 6in (15cm)
Spread: 8in (20cm)
Aspect: Sun
Soil: Sharply-drained, humus-rich
Hardiness: Zone 6
Propagation: Stem-tip cuttings in early summer
Flowering time: Long periods in summer

A semi-evergreen, rounded, perennial. Leaves grayish. Flowers broad funnels, bright yellow, in terminal cymes, borne profusely.

- Drought-tolerant
- Attracts slugs

Linum narbonense (Linaceae)

Common name: Narbonne flax
Height: 2ft (60cm)
Spread: 18in (45cm)
Aspect: Sun
Soil: Sharply-drained
Hardiness: Zone 7
Propagation: Seed, in spring or autumn
Flowering time: Early to midsummer

A short-lived perennial. Flowers rich blue saucers with white eyes, in few-flowered terminal cymes, borne continuously.

- Drought-tolerant
- Attracts slugs
- Must not be moved
- Short-lived

Linum perenne (Linaceae)

Common name: Perennial flax
Height: 2ft (60cm)
Spread: 1ft (30cm)
Aspect: Sun
Soil: Sharply-drained, humus-rich
Hardiness: Zone 5
Propagation: Seed, in spring or autumn
Flowering time: Early to late summer

A lax, straggly species. Leaves glaucous blue-green. Flowers blue, fading to pale blue over the day, cup-shaped, in terminal panicles, borne continuously.

- Drought-tolerant
- Handsome foliage
- Attracts slugs
- Must not be moved

Lobelia erinus (Campanulaceae)

Common name: Edging lobelia
Height: 8in (20cm)
Spread: 6in (15cm)
Aspect: Sun
Soil: Moist, well-drained, fertile
Hardiness: Zone 9
Propagation: Seed as soon as ripe
Flowering time: Summer to autumn

A tender perennial, grown as an annual in cold climates. Flowers two-lipped, tubular, white, pink, red or purple, with yellow or white eyes, in loose racemes.

- Attracts slugs
- Short-lived
- Skin irritant

Linum Gemmell's hybrid A.G.M.

Linum perenne

Linum narbonense

Lobelia erinus

Lobelia x *gerardii* 'Vedrariensis'
(Campanulaceae)

Common name: None
Height: 4ft (1.2m)
Spread: 1ft (30cm)
Aspect: Sun or part shade
Soil: Moist, humus-rich
Hardiness: Zone 7
Propagation: Division, in spring
Flowering time: All summer

A rhizomatous hardy perennial. Leaves in basal rosette. Flowers 2-lipped, tubular, purple, in many-flowered racemes.

- Good cut flower
- Low allergen
- Attracts slugs
- Short-lived
- Skin irritant

Lobularia *maritima* 'Easter Bonnet' series
(Brassicaceae)

Common name: None
Height: 1ft (30cm)
Spread: 1ft (30cm)
Aspect: Full sun
Soil: Well-drained, fertile
Hardiness: Zone 8
Propagation: Seed in situ in late spring
Flowering time: All summer

A short-lived perennial, grown usually as an annual. Leaves gray-green. Flowers white or pink, scented, in corymb-like racemes. Shear over to promote a second flush of flowers.

- Scented flowers
- Short-lived

Lychnis *coronaria* (Caryophyllaceae)

Common name: Rose campion
Height: 32in (80cm)
Spread: 18in (45cm)
Aspect: Sun
Soil: Sharply-drained, fertile
Hardiness: Zone 4
Propagation: Seed or division, in spring
Flowering time: Long period in summer

A short-lived hardy perennial. Leaves woolly silver-gray. Flowers single, scarlet, in small racemes. Deadheading prolongs flowering.

- Drought tolerant
- Good cut flower
- Handsome foliage
- Attracts slugs
- Must deadhead
- Seeds everywhere
- Short-lived

Lobularia maritima 'Easter Bonnet' series

Lychnis coronaria 'Oculata' group

Lychnis *coronaria* 'Oculata' group
(Caryophyllaceae)

Common name: None
Height: 32in (80cm)
Spread: 18in (45cm)
Aspect: Sun
Soil: Sharply-drained, fertile
Hardiness: Zone 4
Propagation: Seed, or division, in spring
Flowering time: Long period in summer

A short-lived hardy perennial. Leaves silver-gray. Flowers single salvers, white, with a pink eye. Deadheading prolongs flowering.

- Drought-tolerant
- Good cut flower
- Handsome foliage
- Attracts slugs
- Must deadhead
- Seeds everywhere
- Short-lived

Lychnis *flos-jovis* 'Hort's variety'
(Caryophyllaceae)

Common name: Flower-of-love
Height: 1ft (30cm)
Spread: 18in (45cm)
Aspect: Sun
Soil: Sharply-drained, fertile
Hardiness: Zone 5
Propagation: Division, in spring
Flowering time: Early to late summer

A hardy perennial. Leaves gray-green. Flowers single, rose-pink, in loosely-rounded cymes.

- Drought-tolerant
- Handsome foliage
- Attracts slugs

Lobelia x gerardii 'Vedrariensis'

Lychnis flos-jovis 'Hort's variety'

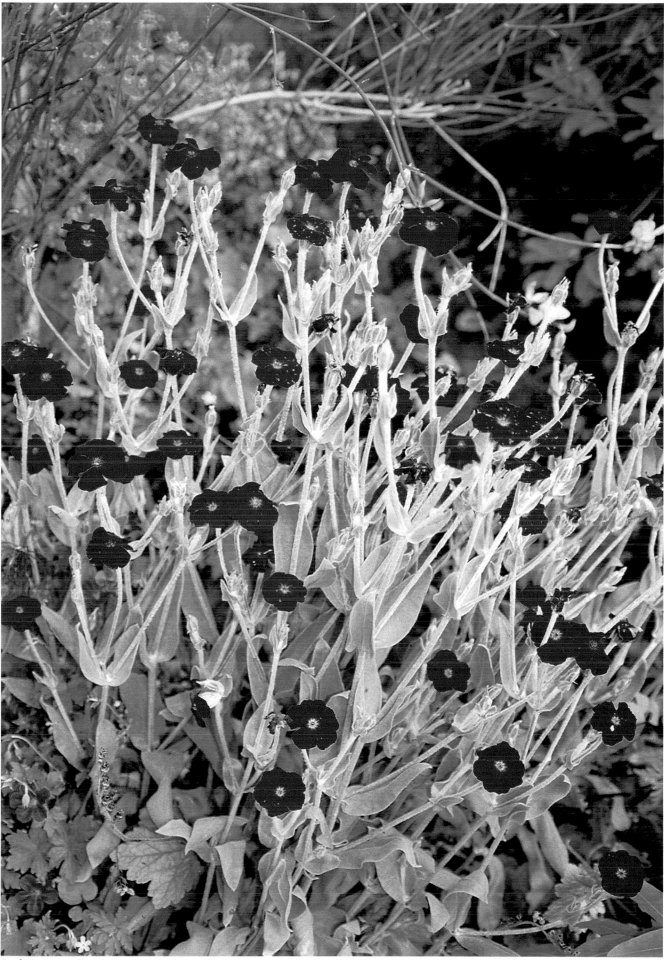

Lychnis coronaria

Malva moschata

Malva sylvestris 'Primley Blue'

Malva sylvestris 'Zebrina'

Matthiola incana 'Brompton' series

Malva moschata (Malvaceae)

Common name: Musk mallow
Height: 3ft (90cm)
Spread: 2ft (60cm)
Aspect: Sun
Soil: Well-drained, moist, fertile
Hardiness: Zone 3
Propagation: Seed or basal cuttings, in spring
Flowering time: Early summer to autumn

A short-lived, woody perennial. Foliage aromatic. Flowers saucer-shaped, pale pink or white in axillary clusters.

- Attracts bees
- Attracts slugs
- Requires staking
- Seeds everywhere
- Short-lived

Malva sylvestris 'Primley Blue' (Malvaceae)

Common name: None
Height: 8in (20cm)
Spread: 2ft (60cm)
Aspect: Sun
Soil: Moist, well-drained, fertile
Hardiness: Zone 5
Propagation: Basal cuttings, in spring
Flowering time: Late spring to mid-autumn

A floppy, hairy, woody, short-lived hardy perennial. Flowers pale blue, with dark blue veining, in axillary clusters.

- Attracts bees
- Seeds everywhere
- Short-lived

Malva sylvestris 'Zebrina' (Malvaceae)

Common name: None
Height: 5ft (1.5m)
Spread: 3ft (90cm)
Aspect: Sun
Soil: Moist, well-drained, fertile
Hardiness: Zone 5
Propagation: Basal cuttings, in spring
Flowering time: Late spring to mid-autumn

A tallish, wide-spreading, woody, short-lived perennial. Flowers in axillary clusters, open funnel-shaped, deep blue-purple, and with darker veins. Very prone to rust.

- Attracts bees
- Requires staking
- Short-lived

Matthiola incana 'Brompton' series (Brassicaceae)

Common name: Common stock
Height: 18in (45cm)
Spread: 9in (23cm)
Aspect: Full sun
Soil: Moist, well-drained, fertile
Hardiness: Zone 6
Propagation: Seed in heat in early spring
Flowering time: Late spring to late summer

A perennial, grown almost always as a biennial. Leaves gray-green. Flowers scented, in upright panicles, single or double, in a range of colors.

- Handsome foliage
- Good cut flower
- Scented flowers

Matthiola incana 'Ten Week' series   *Matthiola* white perennial

Meconopsis cambrica

Meconopsis cambrica var. *aurantiaca* 'FlorePleno'

Matthiola incana 'Ten Week' series (Brassicaceae)

Common name: None
Height: 1ft (30cm)
Spread: 10in (25cm)
Aspect: Full sun
Soil: Moist, well-drained, fertile
Hardiness: Zone 6
Propagation: Seed in heat in early spring
Flowering time: Late spring to late summer

A perennial grown usually as an annual. Foliage gray-green. Flowers scented, single or double, in a range of colors, in panicles.

- Good cut flower
- Handsome foliage
- Scented flowers

Matthiola white perennial (Brassicaceae)

Common name: None
Height: 18in (45cm)
Spread: 1ft (30cm)
Aspect: Sun
Soil: Moist, well-drained, fertile
Hardiness: Zone 7
Propagation: Seed, in spring or autumn
Flowering time: Summer and autumn

A short-lived, woody perennial. Leaves gray-green. Flowers scented, double, white, in terminal spikes.

- Good cut flower   • Short-lived
- Handsome foliage
- Scented flowers

Meconopsis cambrica (Papaveraceae)

Common name: Welsh-poppy
Height: 18in (45cm)
Spread: 1ft (30cm)
Aspect: Any
Soil: Any
Hardiness: Zone 6
Propagation: Seed when ripe
Flowering time: Spring to autumn

A grow-anywhere, tap-rooted perennial. Leaves ferny. Flowers single, solitary, yellow, cup-shaped, on tall stems. Deadhead to prevent self-seeding.

- Handsome foliage   • Attracts slugs
                          • Must not be moved
                          • Prone to mildew
                          • Seeds everywhere

Meconopsis cambrica var. *aurantiaca* 'FlorePleno' (Papaveraceae)

Common name: Orange Welsh-poppy
Height: 18in (45cm)
Spread: 1ft (30cm)
Aspect: Any
Soil: Any
Hardiness: Zone 6
Propagation: Seed when ripe
Flowering time: Spring to autumn

A double orange form of the Welsh poppy, which is reputed not to self-seed to the same degree as the single form. Flower on tallish stems. Deadhead to prevent self-seeding.

- Handsome foliage   • Attracts slugs
                          • Must not be moved
                          • Prone to mildew
                          • Seeds everywhere

Mertensia simplicissima

Mertensia simplicissima (Boraginaceae)

Common name: None
Height: 3ft (90cm)
Spread: 1ft (30cm)
Aspect: Part shade
Soil: Sharply-drained
Hardiness: Zone 6
Propagation: Division in spring; seed in autumn
Flowering time: Late spring to early autumn

A hardy, prostrate perennial. Leaves in rosettes, glaucous blue-green. Flowers tubular, turquoise blue, in terminal cymes on prostrate stems.

- Handsome foliage
- Low allergen
- Attracts slugs
- Must not be moved

MIMULUS *(Scrophulariaceae)*
Monkey-flower

A genus of some 150 species found in damp and sandy areas, so attention has to be paid to their cultural needs. They have snapdragon-like, two-lipped, five-lobed flowers, spotted or bicoloured; these are borne from spring to autumn on upright stems. They are low allergen plants, prone to powdery mildew when young, and attract slugs and snails. *(See also under Shrubs.)*

Mimulus 'Andean Nymph' A.G.M. (Scrophulariaceae)

Common name: Monkey-flower
Height: 8in (20cm)
Spread: 1ft (30cm)
Aspect: Sun or part shade
Soil: Humus-rich, fertile
Hardiness: Zone 6
Propagation: Division in spring; softwood cuttings in early summer
Flowering time: All summer

A rhizomatous, hardy perennial. Flowers trumpet-shaped, white, with cream throats spotted pink, borne on leafy racemes.

- Low allergen
- Attracts slugs
- Prone to mildew
- Short-lived

Mimulus 'Andean Nymph' A.G.M.

Mimulus lewisii A.G.M. (Scrophulariaceae)

Common name: Monkey-flower
Height: 2ft (60cm)
Spread: 18in (45cm)
Aspect: Full sun
Spoil: Well-drained, humus-rich
Hardiness: Zone 5
Propagation: Division, in spring
Flowering time: All summer

A hardy perennial. Flowers axillary, solitary, tubular, deep rose-pink, with cream throats.

- Low allergen
- Attracts slugs
- Mildew-prone
- Short-lived

Mimulus lewisii A.G.M.

Mimulus luteus (Scrophulariaceae)

Common name: Golden monkey-flower
Height: 1ft (30cm)
Spread: 2ft (60cm)
Aspect: Sun or half shade
Soil: Bog or marginal aquatic
Hardiness: Zone 7
Propagation: Seed or division, in spring
Flowering time: Late spring to midsummer

A vigorous, verging on invasive, hardy perennial. Flowers two per axil, yellow, with red-spotted throats and lobes, borne freely. Prolific self-seeder, so deadhead regularly.

- Low allergen
- Attracts slugs
- Prone to mildew
- Seeds everywhere
- Short-lived

Mimulus luteus

Mimulus moschatus

Monarda didyma

Mirabilis jalapa

Nemesia denticulata A.G.M.

Mimulus moschatus (Scrophulariaceae)

Common name: None
Height: 1ft (30cm)
Spread: 1ft (30cm)
Aspect: Sun or part shade
Soil: Wet or marginal aquatic
Hardiness: Zone 7
Propagation: Seed or division, in spring
Flowering time: Summer to autumn

A creeping, marginal aquatic perennial. Flowers pale yellow, spotted and blotched dark brown. Scented of musk.

- Low allergen
- Scented flowers
- Attracts slugs
- Prone to mildew
- Short-lived

Mirabilis jalapa (Nyctaginaceae)

Common name: Common four-o'clock
Height: 2ft (60cm)
Spread: 2ft (60cm)
Aspect: Sun, no winter wet
Soil: Well-drained, fertile
Hardiness: Zone 8
Propagation: Seed in warmth, or division, in spring
Flowering time: Early to late summer

A tuberous, half-hardy perennial. Flowers scented, in several colors, often present on the plant at the same time, lasting from only late afternoon to night.

- Scented flowers
- Attracts slugs

Monarda didyma (Lamiaceae)

Common name: Bee-balm
Height: 3ft (90cm)
Spread: 18in (45cm)
Aspect: Sun or part shade
Soil: Moist, well-drained, fertile
Hardiness: Zone 4
Propagation: Division, or basal cuttings, in spring
Flowering time: Mid- to late summer

A hardy perennial. Leaves aromatic. Flowers on long stems, each bearing two whorls of pink 2-lipped, sage-like, tubular flowers. Deadhead to prolong flowering.

- Attracts bees
- Good cut flower
- Low allergen
- Attracts slugs
- Prone to mildew
- Requires staking

Nemesia denticulata A.G.M. (Scrophulariaceae)

Common name: None
Height: 16in (40cm)
Spread: 8in (20cm)
Aspect: Sun
Soil: Acidic, moist, well-drained, fertile
Hardiness: Zone 8
Propagation: Seed in heat, in spring or autumn
Flowering time: All summer

A neat, compact half-hardy perennial. Flowers scented, of smoky pink, with a yellow eye.

- Scented flowers

NEPETA (Lamiaceae)
Nepeta

A genus of some 250 species, from a wide range of habitats, from hot and dry to cool and moist. The flowers are tubular, two-lipped, in white and blue, sometimes yellow; they are borne in cymes, for long periods in the case of the plants featured here. The foliage may be aromatic, and cats love to make a bed of it. The plant also attracts bees.

Nepetas vary in their requirements, so see details of the individual plants. They are prone to powdery mildew, and slug damage.

Nepeta longipes (Lamiaceae)

Common name: None
Height: 2ft (60cm)
Spread: 18in (45cm)
Aspect: Sun or part shade
Soil: Well-drained
Hardiness: Zone 5
Propagation: Division, spring or autumn
Flowering time: Many weeks in summer

A hardy perennial. Leaves aromatic, toothed, gray-green. Flowers on tallish upright stems, lilac-blue, in close whorls.

- Attracts bees
- Drought-tolerant
- Low allergen
- Attracts slugs
- Prone to mildew

Nepeta 'Six Hills Giant' (Lamiaceae)

Common name: None
Height: 3ft (90cm)
Spread: 2ft (60cm)
Aspect: Sun or part shade
Soil: Well-drained
Hardiness: Zone 3
Propagation: Division, spring or autumn
Flowering time: All summer

A vigorous, hardy perennial. Leaves aromatic, hairy, gray-green. Flowers abundant, lavender-blue, in spiky, whorled cymes.

- Attracts bees
- Drought-tolerant
- Low allergen
- Attracts slugs
- Prone to mildew
- Requires staking

Nepeta subsessilis (Lamiaceae)

Common name: None
Height: 3ft (90cm)
Spread: 1ft (30cm)
Aspect: Sun or part shade
Soil: Well-drained
Hardiness: Zone 7
Propagation: Division, spring or autumn
Flowering time: Midsummer to early autumn

A clump-forming perennial. Leaves aromatic, toothed, deep green. Flowers bright blue, in whorled cymes.

- Attracts bees
- Drought-tolerant
- Low allergen
- Attracts slugs
- Prone to mildew
- Requires staking

Nepeta tuberosa (Lamiaceae)

Common name: None
Height: 3ft (90cm)
Spread: 1ft (30cm)
Aspect: Sun or part shade
Soil: Well-drained
Hardiness: Zone 8
Propagation: Seed in autumn; division, spring or autumn
Flowering time: Several weeks in summer

A tender, tuberous perennial. Leaves green, aromatic. Flowers violet-purple, in a spike.

- Attracts bees
- Drought-tolerant
- Low allergen
- Attracts slugs
- Prone to mildew
- Requires staking

Nepeta longipes

Nepeta 'Six Hills Giant'

Nepeta subsessilis

Nepeta tuberosa

Nerine bowdenii A.G.M.

Nerine bowdenii A.G.M. (Amaryllidaceae)

Common name: Cape colony nerine
Height: 18in (45cm)
Spread: 4in (10cm)
Aspect: Sun
Soil: Well-drained, fertile
Hardiness: Zone 8
Propagation: Seed in heat when ripe;
division, after flowering
Flowering time: Several weeks in autumn

A half-hardy, bulbous perennial. Leaves strap-like, green. Flowers very weather-resistant, scented, pink, funnel-shaped, with recurved tepals, in open umbels of up to 7.

- Drought-tolerant
- Good cut flower
- Scented flowers
- Attracts slugs
- Poisonous

Nicotiana x *sanderae* 'Havana Appleblossom'

NICOTIANA (Solanaceae)
Nicotiana

A genus of over 60 species of plants from usually moist sites in tropical areas. The flowers are tubular, or trumpet-shaped, may be scented, and are borne in panicles or racemes over long periods in summer and perhaps into autumn. The flowers open during the evening or at night, but may open during the day in shade.
Nicotiana like moist, but well-drained soil, and sun or part shade. They may require to be staked. Perennial species can be over-wintered outside in warm areas.
(See also under Annuals.)

Nicotiana 'Roulette' series

Nicotiana sylvestris A.G.M.

Nicotiana x *sanderae* 'Havana Appleblossom' (Solanaceae)

Common name: None
Height: 15in (38cm)
Spread: 1ft (30cm)
Aspect: Sun or part shade
Soil: Moist, well-drained, fertile
Hardiness: Zone 7
Propagation: Seed in heat in spring
Flowering time: Early to late summer

An upright, dwarf, short-lived perennial, grown usually as an annual. Flowers open salvers of white or pale pink, in panicles.

- Scented flowers
- Short-lived
- Skin irritant

Nicotiana 'Roulette' series (Solanaceae)

Common name: None
Height: 10in (25cm)
Spread: 9in (23cm)
Aspect: Sun or part shade
Soil: Moist, well-drained, fertile
Hardiness: Zone 8
Propagation: Seed in heat in spring
Flowering time: All summer

An upright, short-lived perennial, grown usually as an annual. Flowers open salvers, in a range of colors, and bicolored, in panicles.

- Scented flowers
- Short-lived
- Skin irritant

Nicotiana sylvestris A.G.M. (Solanaceae)

Common name: None
Height: 5ft (1.5m)
Spread: 2ft (60cm)
Aspect: Part shade
Soil: Moist, well-drained
Hardiness: Zone 8
Propagation: Seed in heat in spring
Flowering time: All summer

A robust, short-lived perennial. Flowers nodding, perfumed, long trumpets, white, in densely-packed panicles; closed in full sun.

- Scented flowers
- Short-lived
- Skin irritant

Oenothera fruticosa

Oenothera glazioviana

Oenothera macrocarpa A.G.M.

Oenothera nuttallii

OENOTHERA (Onagraceae)
Oenothera

A genus of some 150 species of perennials, biennials, and annuals. They grow invariably on well-drained soils such as mountain slopes and deserts. Whilst many are nocturnal-flowering, not all are. The individual flowers last only one day or night, but flowers are borne in a long succession over many weeks in summer. Yellow is the predominant color in the genus, but some are pink, others white. The flowers may be perfumed in some types. Some are tap-rooted and therefore do not survive transplantation; many are short-lived.

Oenothera fruticosa (Onagraceae)

Common name: Common sundrops
Height: 3ft (90cm)
Spread: 1ft (30cm)
Aspect: Full sun
Soil: Sharply-drained
Hardiness: Zone 4
Propagation: Division, in early spring
Flowering time: Late spring to late summer

A short-lived perennial. Flowers diurnal, cup-shaped, dark yellow, in racemes of up to 10.

- Attract bees
- Drought-tolerant
- Good cut flower
- Attracts slugs
- Must not be moved
- Seeds everywhere
- Short-lived

Oenothera glazioviana (Onagraceae)

Common name: None
Height: 5ft (1.5m)
Spread: 2ft (60cm)
Aspect: Sun
Soil: Sharply-drained
Hardiness: Zone 3
Propagation: Seed in spring
Flowering time: Mid- and late summer

A short-lived perennial. Leaves in a basal rosette. Flowers large, bowl-shaped, yellow, nocturnal, in racemes.

- Attracts bees
- Drought-tolerant
- Good cut flower
- Attracts slugs
- Must not be moved
- Seeds everywhere
- Short-lived

Oenothera macrocarpa A.G.M. (Onagraceae)

Common name: None
Height: 6in (15cm)
Spread: 2ft (60cm)
Aspect: Sun
Soil: Sharply-drained
Hardiness: Zone 5
Propagation: Seed in spring
Flowering time: Late spring to early autumn

A prostrate, herbaceous perennial. Flowers large, solitary, golden yellow, opening in daytime.

- Attracts bees
- Drought-tolerant
- Attracts slugs
- Must not be moved

Oenothera nuttallii (Onagraceae)

Common name: None
Height: 1ft (30cm)
Spread: 3ft (90cm)
Aspect: Sun
Soil: Sharply-drained
Hardiness: Zone 5
Propagation: Seed, in early spring
Flowering time: Late summer to late autumn

A prostrate, hardy, herbaceous perennial, late to restart growth (midsummer), so mark the position well. Flowers very large, pale lemon-yellow.

- Attracts bees
- Drought-tolerant
- Attracts slugs
- Must not be moved

Oenothera speciosa 'Siskyou'

Omphalodes cappadocica 'Starry Eyes'

Origanum laevigatum 'Herrenhausen'

Osteospermum jucundum var. *compactum*

Oenothera speciosa 'Siskyou' (Onagraceae)

Common name: Showy evening-primrose
Height: 1ft (30cm)
Spread: 1ft (30cm)
Aspect: Full sun
Soil: Sharply-drained
Hardiness: Zone 5
Propagation: Division, in spring
Flowering time: Early summer to autumn

A low-growing, short-lived, hardy perennial. Very choice clone. Flowers pink, with yellow centers. May be invasive.

- Attracts bees
- Attracts slugs
- Drought-tolerant
- Must not be moved

Omphalodes cappadocica 'Starry Eyes' (Boraginaceae)

Common name: None
Height: 1ft (30cm)
Spread: 18in (45cm)
Aspect: Part shade
Soil: Moist, humus-rich
Hardiness: Zone 6
Propagation: Division, in spring
Flowering time: Many weeks in early spring

An evergreen, woodland perennial. Flowers small, blue, with a white eye, and a central white stripe on each petal, in loose racemes. *Omphalodes* 'Cherry Ingram' is very similar, with unmarked blue flowers.

- Evergreen
- Attracts slugs
- Low allergen

Origanum laevigatum 'Herrenhausen' A.G.M. (Lamiaceae)

Common name: None
Height: 18in (45cm)
Spread: 18in (45cm)
Aspect: Sun
Soil: Well drained, fertile
Hardiness: Zone 8
Propagation: Division, or basal cuttings, in spring
Flowering time: Late spring to autumn

An evergreen, half-hardy perennial. Leaves aromatic, purple-green. Flowers deep pink, tubular, in dense panicle-like whorls, and surrounded by purple-red bracts.

- Attracts bees
- Drought-tolerant
- Evergreen

Osteospermum jucundum var. *compactum* A.G.M. (Asteraceae)

Common name: None
Height: 8in (20cm)
Spread: 3ft (90cm)
Aspect: Full sun
Soil: Well-drained, humus-rich
Hardiness: Zone 7
Propagation: Seed in heat, in spring
Flowering time: Early summer to autumn

A hardy, prostrate, evergreen perennial. Flowers single, solitary, with mauve ray florets and yellow disc florets.

- Evergreen
- Highly allergenic
- Good cut flower
- Must deadhead

Papaver spicatum (Papaveraceae)

Common name: Poppy
Height: 2ft (60cm)
Spread: 6in (15cm)
Aspect: Sun
Soil: Well-drained, fertile
Hardiness: Zone 8
Propagation: Seed, in spring
Flowering time: Several weeks in summer

A perennial with pale green leaves in a basal rosette. Flowers in a slender raceme, pale orange, outward-facing.

- Low allergen
- Must not be moved

Passiflora caerulea A.G.M. (Passifloraceae)

Common name: Passion-flower
Height: 30ft (9m)
Spread: 3ft (90cm)
Aspect: Sun or part shade
Soil: Moist, well-drained, fertile
Hardiness: Zone 7
Propagation: Layer in spring or autumn; semi-ripe cuttings in summer
Flowering time: Summer to autumn

The only hardy Passion-flower. A vigorous, spreading climber. Flowers flat, white, with coronas zoned in purple, blue, and white; edible fruits. Prune for size and shape, and cut out crowded shoots in early spring.

- Evergreen
- Low allergen
- Invasive
- Requires space

Passiflora quadrangularis A.G.M. (Passifloraceae)

Common name: Passion-flower
Height: 50ft (15m)
Spread: 3ft (90cm)
Aspect: Sun or part shade
Soil: Moist, well-drained, fertile
Hardiness: Zone 10
Propagation: Layer in spring or autumn; semi-ripe cuttings in summer
Flowering time: Midsummer to autumn

A tuberous, vigorous climber. Flowers scented, pendent, red, with large coronas of purple filaments, banded red; followed by edible fruits. Prune for shape and size, as and when needed.

- Evergreen
- Low allergen
- Scented flowers
- Requires space

PELARGONIUM (Geraniaceae)
Pelargonium

A genus of about 230 species, but the many thousands of commercial cultivars are derived from only a handful of species. They are mostly of South African origin, and all are Zone 9 or 10 (with the single exception of *P. endlicherianum*, which is Zone 7). They flower all year round in warm climates, but only over the summer in cool countries, unless they are given protection from the winter cold in a warm greenhouse or conservatory. There are three major groups of flowering pelargoniums:

Zonal pelargoniums This, the largest group, comprises evergreen perennials, many with variegated foliage, and can be divided further into six subclasses, depending on flower shape and size, but for the purpose of this book can be regarded as belonging to two main groups: a) those raised from seed for bedding out, are single-flowered, and come true from seed, and b) large-flowered cultivars raised from cuttings and which can be bedded out but which also make excellent house or conservatory plants during the winter in cold counties. The blooms of double-flowered cultivars of this group, in particular, can be spoiled by rain.

Regal pelargoniums This group is also evergreen, but may be perennial or shrubby.

Ivy-leaved pelargoniums These are evergreen, trailing perennials, and make excellent hanging basket plants.

Contact with the foliage of pelargoniums may cause, or exacerbate, skin problems, and the plants are highly allergenic. Routine deadheading is important in keeping pelargoniums flowering continuously.

There are specialist nurseries, societies, and books devoted to the pelargonium, and the reader who requires further in-depth information should consult these.

Pelargonium endlicherianum (Geraniaceae)

Common name: None
Height: 10in (25cm)
Spread: 6in (15cm)
Aspect: Full sun, no winter wet
Soil: Sharply-drained
Hardiness: Zone 7
Propagation: Seed in heat, in spring
Flowering time: Many weeks in summer

The only hardy Pelargonium. Leaves basal, crenate, dark green. Flowers deep pink, veined purple, in tall scapes. Dislikes winter wet.

- Highly allergenic
- Must deadhead
- Skin irritant

Passiflora quadrangularis A.G.M.

Papaver spicatum

Passiflora caerulea A.G.M.

Pelargonium endlicherianum

Pelargonium peltatum

Pelargonium regale hybridus

Pelargonium tricolor (= 'Splendide')

Pelargonium peltatum (Geraniaceae)

Common name: None
Height: 8in (20cm)
Spread: 3ft (90cm)
Aspect: Sun, no winter wet
Soil: Well-drained, fertile
Hardiness: Zone 10
Propagation: Seed in heat, or softwood cuttings in spring
Flowering time: All summer

An evergreen, prostrate, or trailing, tender perennial. Leaves stiff, lobed, pointed, green. Flowers single or double, in shades of pink, red, white, orange, reddish-black, or purple.

- Evergreen
- Highly allergenic
- Must deadhead
- Skin irritant

Pelargonium regale hybridus (Geraniaceae)

Common name: None
Height: 1ft (30cm)
Spread: 10in (25cm)
Aspect: Part shade, no winter wet
Soil: Well-drained, fertile
Hardiness: Zone 9
Propagation: Seed in heat, or softwood cuttings, in spring
Flowering time: All summer

Bushy, evergreen perennials or subshrubs. Leaves rounded, mid-green. Flowers single, rarely double, in clusters, in red, pink, purple, white, orange, or reddish-black, or bicolored. Likes half shade. Whitefly prone.

- Evergreen
- Highly allergenic
- Must deadhead
- Skin irritant

Pelargonium tricolor (= 'Splendide') (Geraniaceae)

Common name: None
Height: 1ft (30cm)
Spread: 8in (20cm)
Aspect: Sun
Soil: Moist, well-drained
Hardiness: Zone 9
Propagation: Softwood cuttings in spring to autumn
Flowering time: Several weeks in summer

A tender perennial. Leaves hairy, deeply-cut, gray-green. Flowers with red upper petals, with a black base, and white lower petals.

- Evergreen
- Highly allergenic
- Must deadhead
- Skin irritant

Pelargonium zonale hybridus (= cultorum) (Geraniaceae)

Common name: None
Height: 2ft (60cm)
Spread: 1ft (30cm)
Aspect: Sun or part shade; no winter wet
Soil: Moist, well-drained
Hardiness: Zone 9
Propagation: Softwood cuttings in spring, summer or autumn
Flowering time: All summer

Bushy evergreen perennials. Leaves rounded, hairy, green or zoned bronze/maroon. Flowers single or double, red, pink, purple, white, or orange. Deadhead regularly.

- Evergreen
- Highly allergenic
- Must deadhead
- Skin irritant

Pelargonium zonale hybridus (= cultorum)

63

Penstemon 'Flamingo'

Penstemon heterophyllus 'Blue Springs'

Penstemon 'Osprey' A.G.M.

Penstemon 'Rosy Blush'

Penstemon heterophyllus 'Blue Springs' (Scrophulariaceae)

Common name: Chaparral penstemon
Height: 20in (50cm)
Spread: 20in (50cm)
Aspect: Sun or part shade
Soil: Well-drained
Hardiness: Zone 8
Propagation: Division, in spring
Flowering time: Several weeks in summer

An evergreen. Leaves bluish-green. Flowers tubular, blue, with lilac lobes, in racemes.

- Evergreen
- Handsome foliage
- Low allergen
- Attracts slugs
- Must deadhead
- Prone to mildew

Penstemon 'Osprey' A.G.M. (Scrophulariaceae)

Common name: None
Height: 3ft (90cm)
Spread: 18in (45cm)
Aspect: Sun or part shade
Soil: Well-drained, fertile
Hardiness: Zone 7
Propagation: Division, in spring
Flowering time: Early summer to autumn

A tall hybrid. Flowers tubular, rose-carmine, with a white throat, in racemes.

- Low allergen
- Attracts slugs
- Must deadhead
- Prone to mildew
- Requires staking

Penstemon 'Rosy Blush' (Scrophulariaceae)

Common name: None
Height: 3ft (90cm)
Spread: 18in (45cm)
Aspect: Sun or part shade
Soil: Well-drained, fertile
Hardiness: Zone 8
Propagation: Division, in spring
Flowering time: Early to late summer

A hybrid perennial. Flowers tubular or bell-shaped, pink, with a white interior, and violet mouth, in one-sided racemes.

- Low allergen
- Attracts slugs
- Must deadhead
- Prone to mildew

PENSTEMON (Scrophulariaceae)
Penstemon

A genus of about 250 species, but many hundreds more hybrids. They can be evergreen or deciduous. They are mostly half-hardy, but some are hardy. The foxglove-like flowers may be tubular, bell-shaped or funnel-shaped, and are borne in panicles or racemes from early summer to mid-autumn.

Penstemons like sun or part shade, and a soil which is well-drained, and not over fertile; they do not flower well or overwinter well, if overfed. They should be given a shear over after flowering, and a dry mulch over winter in cold regions. They are prone to slug damage and powdery mildew.
(See also under Shrubs.)

Penstemon 'Flamingo' (Scrophulariaceae)

Common name: None
Height: 3ft (90cm)
Spread: 1ft (30cm)
Aspect: Sun or half shade
Soil: Well-drained
Hardiness: Zone 7
Propagation: Division in spring
Flowering time: Early summer to mid-autumn

A hybrid semi-evergreen perennial. Flowers tubular, white with pink margins, in racemes.

- Low allergen
- Attracts slugs
- Must deadhead
- Prone to mildew

Penstemon 'Sour Grapes'

Penstemon 'Sour Grapes'
(Scrophulariaceae)

Common name: None
Height: 2ft (60cm)
Spread: 18in (45cm)
Aspect: Sun or part shade
Soil: Well-drained, fertile
Hardiness: Zone 6
Propagation: Division, in spring
Flowering time: Midsummer to mid-autumn

A half-hardy perennial. Flowers tubular, or bell-shaped, dull lilac-blue, with white throats, in one-sided racemes.

- Low allergen
- Attracts slugs
- Must deadhead
- Prone to mildew

Petrea volubilis (Verbenaceae)

Common name: None
Height: 40ft (12m)
Spread: 5ft (1.5m)
Aspect: Full sun
Soil: Moist, well-drained, fertile
Hardiness: Zone 10
Propagation: Semi-ripe cuttings with bottom heat in summer
Flowering time: Late winter to summer

A semi-evergreen climber. Flowers salverform, amethyst blue, in arching panicles. Prune for size and shape after flowering.

- Requires space

Petrea volubilis

Petunia x *hybrida* 'Prism Sunshine' series

Petunia x *hybrida* 'Prism Sunshine' series
(Solanaceae)

Common name: Garden petunia
Height: 10in (25cm)
Spread 15in (38cm)
Aspect: Full sun
Soil: Well-drained
Hardiness: Zone 7
Propagation: Softwood cuttings in spring
Flowering time: Late spring to late autumn

A free-flowering perennial, grown invariably as an annual. Flowers large, yellow, veined, fade-resistant. Deadheading prolongs flowering.

- Low allergen
- Attracts slugs
- Must deadhead

Petunia x *hybrida* 'Summer Morn' series
(Solanaceae)

Common name: Garden petunia
Height: 1ft (30cm)
Spread: 18in (45cm)
Aspect: Sun
Soil: Well-drained
Hardiness: Zone 7
Propagation: Softwood cuttings in spring
Flowering time: Late spring to late autumn

A compact, free-flowering perennial, grown as an annual. Flowers large, in a range of colors, self-colored, or throated in a paler color. Deadheading prolongs flowering.

- Low allergen
- Attracts slugs
- Must deadhead

Petunia x *hybrida* 'Summer Morn' series

Petunia x *hybrida* 'Surfinia' series

Petunia x *hybrida* 'Ultra' series

Phlox 'Chattahoochee' A.G.M.

Phuopsis stylosa

Petunia x *hybrida* 'Surfinia' series (Solanaceae)

Common name: Garden petunia
Height: 16in (40cm)
Spread: 3ft (90cm)
Aspect: Full sun
Soil: Well-drained
Hardiness: Zone 7
Propagation: Softwood cuttings in spring
Flowering time: Late spring to late autumn

A grandiflora petunia, of trailing habit, ideal for hanging baskets. Perennial, but invariably grown as an annual. Flowers large, in shades of blue, lavender, pink, or magenta. Must be deadheaded.

- Low allergen
- Attracts slugs
- Must deadhead

Petunia x *hybrida* 'Ultra' series (Solanaceae)

Common name: Garden petunia
Height: 1ft (30cm)
Spread: 3ft (90cm)
Aspect: Full sun
Soil: Well-drained
Hardiness: Zone 7
Propagation: Seed in heat in spring
Flowering time: Late spring to autumn

A grandiflora petunia. Perennial, but almost always grown as an annual. Flowers large, in very many colors, with central white stars. Weather-resistant.

- Low allergen
- Attracts slugs
- Must deadhead

Phlox 'Chattahoochee' A.G.M. (Polemoniaceae)

Common name: None
Height: 6in (15cm)
Spread: 1ft (30cm)
Aspect: Half shade
Soil: Moist, well-drained, humus-rich, fertile
Hardiness: Zone 4
Propagation: Softwood cuttings of blind shoots, in spring
Flowering time: Summer to early autumn

A short-lived, prostrate perennial. Flowers salveriform, lavender-blue, with a red eye, in cymes.

- Low allergen
- Attracts slugs
- Prone to mildew
- Short-lived

Phuopsis stylosa (Rubiaceae)

Common name: None
Height: 6in (15cm)
Spread: 3ft (90cm)
Aspect: Sun or part shade
Soil: Moist, sharply-drained, fertile
Hardiness: Zone 7
Propagation: Seed in autumn; division, spring or autumn
Flowering time: All summer

A mat-forming, sprawling perennial. Leaves musk-scented. Flowers scented, small, pink, in dense globular heads. Shear over after flowering to keep compact.

- Scented flowers
- Seeds everywhere

Podranea ricasoliana (Bignoniaceae)

Common name: None
Height: 15ft (4.5m)
Spread: 3ft (90cm)
Aspect: Part shade
Soil: Moist, well-drained, fertile
Hardiness: Zone 9
Propagation: Seed in heat, or layer, in spring
Flowering time: Winter to summer

An evergreen climber. Flowers in panicles of up to 12, pink. Prune just after flowering by cutting back to within 3 to 4 buds of permanent framework. Tender.

- Evergreen
- Requires space

Podranea ricasoliana

Potentilla nepalensis 'Miss Willmott' A.G.M. (Rosaceae)

Common name: Nepal cinquefoil
Height: 18in (45cm)
Spread: 2ft (60cm)
Aspect: Sun
Soil: Well-drained
Hardiness: Zone 5
Propagation: Division, in spring or autumn
Flowering time: All summer

Hardy; clumpforming. Flowers flat, cherry-red, with dark pink centers, in loose cymes.

● Attracts bees
● Low allergen

Potentilla 'William Rollison' A.G.M. (Rosaceae)

Common name: None
Height: 18in (45cm)
Spread: 2ft (60cm)
Aspect: Sun
Soil: Well-drained
Hardiness: Zone 5
Propagation: Division, in spring or autumn
Flowering time: Early to late summer

A hardy, clump-forming perennial. Flowers flat, semi-double, orange-red, in cymes.

● Attracts bees
● Low allergen

Pratia pedunculata (Campanulaceae)

Common name: None
Height: 1in (2.5cm)
Spread: Indefinite
Aspect: Shade
Soil: Well-drained, humus-rich
Hardiness: Zone 7
Propagation: Division, at any time of year
Flowering time: Long periods in summer

A creeping, mat-forming perennial. Flowers almost stemless, small, star-shaped, deep blue.

● Attracts slugs
● Invasive

Pulmonaria rubra 'Bowles Red' (Boraginaceae)

Common name: None
Height: 16in (45cm)
Spread: 3ft (90cm)
Aspect: Shade, part or full
Soil: Moist, humus-rich, fertile
Hardiness: Zone 5
Propagation: Division, after flowering, or in autumn
Flowering time: Late winter to mid-spring

A rhizomatous, evergreen, creeping perennial. Leaves have pale green spots. Flowers funnel-shaped, coral-red, in cymes. Good ground cover in shade.

● Attracts bees   ● Attracts slugs
● Evergreen   ● Prone to mildew
● Handsome foliage   ● Seeds everywhere
● Low allergen

Potentilla nepalensis 'Miss Willmott' A.G.M.   *Potentilla* 'William Rollison' A.G.M.

Pratia pedunculata

Pulmonaria rubra 'Bowles Red'

Pulmonaria saccharata (Boraginaceae)

Common name: Bethlehem sage
Height: 1ft (30cm)
Spread: 2ft (60cm)
Aspect: Part or full shade
Soil: Moist, humus-rich, fertile
Hardiness: Zone 3
Propagation: Seed when ripe; division, late spring or autumn
Flowering time: Late winter to late spring

A rhizomatous, evergreen perennial. Leaves green, spotted white. Flowers funnel-shaped, red, or white, in cymes. Good ground cover.

- Evergreen
- Handsome foliage
- Low allergen
- Attracts slugs
- Prone to mildew
- Seeds everywhere

Rehmannia elata (Scrophulariaceae)

Common name: Beverly-bells rehmannia
Height: 4ft (1.2m)
Spread: 20in (50cm)
Aspect: Sun; no winter wet
Soil: Well-drained, humus-rich, fertile
Hardiness: Zone 9
Propagation: Seed in warmth, or separate runners, in early spring
Flowering time: Summer to autumn

A tender perennial, grown as a biennial in cold areas. Flowers tubular, semi-pendent, pink, with spotted throats, in racemes. *Rehmannia glutinosa* A.G.M. is very similar.

- Drought-tolerant
- Attracts slugs
- Short-lived

Rhodochiton atrosanguineus (Scrophulariaceae)

Common name: None
Height: 10ft (3m)
Spread: 1ft (30cm)
Aspect: Full sun
Soil: Moist, well-drained, fertile
Hardiness: Zone 9
Propagation: Seed in heat when ripe, or in spring
Flowering time: Summer to autumn

A tender climber. Leaves heart-shaped, green, veined/marbled red. Flowers pendent, solitary, tubular, black, or deep purple, with long-tubed corollas.

- Handsome foliage

Rehmannia elata

Rhodohypoxis baurii var. confecta (Hypoxidaceae)

Common name: None
Height: 4in (10cm)
Spread: 4in (10cm)
Aspect: Sun; no winter wet
Soil: Sharply-drained, humus-rich, fertile
Hardiness: Zone 8
Propagation: Seed, in heat when ripe; offsets in autumn
Flowering time: All summer

A cormous perennial. Leaves grayish-green. Flowers solitary, flat, pink. Dislikes winter wet and in such areas grow *R. milloides*.

- Drought-tolerant
- Handsome foliage

Rhodochiton atrosanguineus

Pulmonaria saccharata

Rhodohypoxis baurii var. *confecta*

Roscoea purpurea (Zingiberaceae)

Common name: None
Height: 3ft (90cm)
Spread: 3ft (90cm)
Aspect: Part shade
Soil: Moist, well-drained, humus-rich, fertile
Hardiness: Zone 6
Propagation: Seed when ripe; division, in spring
Flowering time: Long period in late summer and early autumn

A tuberous, herbaceous perennial which does not reappear till midsummer, so mark the position well. Flowers hooded, purple.

- Low allergen
- Attracts slugs
- Requires staking

Rudbeckia 'Herbstonne' (Asteraceae)

Common name: None
Height: 6ft (1.8m)
Spread: 4ft (1.2m)
Aspect: Sun or part shade
Soil: Well-drained, humus-rich, fertile
Hardiness: Zone 3
Propagation: Division, in spring or autumn
Flowering time: Late summer to late autumn

A tall, invasive hardy rhizomatous perennial. Flowers single, solitary, yellow daisies, with prominent dark centers. Superb cut flower, lasting weeks.

- Attracts bees
- Good cut flower
- Highly allergenic
- Requires space
- Requires staking

Rudbeckia hirta 'Rustic Dwarf' strain (Asteraceae)

Common name: Black-eyed Susan
Height: 2ft (60cm)
Spread: 18in (45cm)
Aspect: Sun or part shade
Soil: Well-drained, humus-rich, fertile
Hardiness: Zone 4
Propagation: Seed in early spring
Flowering time: Summer to late autumn

A dwarf strain of an erect, short-lived perennial, grown as an annual in cold climates. Flowers single, solitary, yellow daisies, with dark central boss.

- Attracts bees
- Good cut flower
- Attracts slugs
- Short-lived

RUDBECKIA (Asteraceae)
Rudbeckia

A genus of only some 20 species of annuals and perennials. The flowers are daisy-like, solitary, usually single, with yellow or orange ray florets, and brown or black disc florests in a cone. They are borne on long stems for a long period from summer to autumn. They like sun or part shade, and a soil which is moist and does not dry out. Some perennial species such as *R. hirta* are often grown as annuals. Slugs are fond of the genus.

Rudbeckia fulgida var. sullivantii 'Goldsturm' A.G.M. (Asteraceae)

Common name: Showy coneflower
Height: 2ft (60cm)
Spread: 18in (45cm)
Aspect: Sun or part shade
Soil: Well-drained, humus-rich, fertile
Hardiness: Zone 4
Propagation: Division, in spring or autumn
Flowering time: Late summer to mid-autumn

A rhizomatous, hardy perennial. Flowers solitary, single, yellow daisies, with a raised, black center.

- Attracts bees
- Good cut flower
- Attracts slugs
- Highly allergenic

Rudbeckia hirta 'Rustic Dwarf' strain

Roscoea purpurea

Rudbeckia fulgida var. *sullivantii*

Rudbeckia 'Herbstonne'

Rudbeckia laciniata 'Goldquelle' A.G.M.

Rudbeckia maxima

Rudbeckia subtomentosa

Saintpaulia ionantha

Rudbeckia laciniata 'Goldquelle' A.G.M. (Asteraceae)

Common name: None
Height: 3ft (90cm)
Spread: 18in (45cm)
Aspect: Sun or part shade
Soil: Well-drained, humus-rich
Hardiness: Zone 3
Propagation: Division, in spring or autumn
Flowering time: Summer to autumn

A rhizomatous, compact, hardy perennial. Flowers solitary, double, lemon-yellow, becoming yellow with age, and green centers.

- Attracts bees
- Good cut flower
- Attracts slugs
- Highly allergenic

Rudbeckia maxima (Asteraceae)

Common name: Great coneflower
Height: 5ft (1.5m)
Spread: 3ft (90cm)
Aspect: Sun or part shade
Soil: Well-drained, humus-rich, fertile
Hardiness: Zone 7
Propagation: Seed, or division, in spring
Flowering time: Late summer to mid-autumn

Hardy. Flowers solitary, single, yellow daisies with prominent dark central cones.

- Attracts bees
- Good cut flower
- Highly allergenic
- Requires staking

Rudbeckia subtomentosa (Asteraceae)

Common name: Sweet coneflower
Height: 28in (70cm)
Spread: 2ft (60cm)
Aspect: Sun or part shade
Soil: Well-drained, humus-rich, fertile
Hardiness: Zone 5
Propagation: Seed, or division, in spring
Flowering time: Late summer to mid-autumn

A hardy perennial. Flowers solitary, single, yellow daisies, with dark brown centers.

- Attracts bees
- Good cut flower
- Highly allergenic

Saintpaulia ionantha (Gesneriaceae)

Common name: None
Height: 4in (10cm)
Spread: 8in (20cm)
Aspect: Sun, but not in summer
Soil: Sharply-drained
Hardiness: Zone 10
Propagation: Seed in heat, when ripe, or in spring
Flowering time: All year (provided there are 12 hours of daylight or fluorescent light and with temperature not below 18°C)

A tender perennial. Leaves in rosettes, gray-green. Flowers blue, in cymes.

- Handsome foliage
- Prone to mildew

Salvia africana-lutea

Salvia coccinea

Salvia farinacea 'Snowball'

Salvia nemorosa 'Pusztaflamme' A.G.M.

SALVIA (Lamiaceae)
Salvia

A genus of about 900 species from temperate and tropical regions, and a wide range of habitats. They may be annual, biennial, or perennial; they include species that are subshrubs, evergreen, or deciduous, fully hardy or tender. The foliage is handsome, and may be aromatic. The flowers are two-lipped: the upper petal is a hood, and the lower is forked. Calyces and bracts may be colored. The flowers are borne in axillary whorls or panicles, on tall stems, over long periods in summer and autumn.

Cultivation requirements vary, but in general, Salvias like moist, humus-rich, well-drained fertile soil in part shade. Those species with woolly or hairy leaves require full sun and sharp drainage, and protection from winter wet and cold, drying winds. Salvias are low-allergen, but prone to slug damage. The tall varieties require to be staked.

Salvia africana-lutea (Lamiaceae)

Common name: None
Height: 3ft (90cm)
Spread: 3ft (90cm)
Aspect: Sun
Soil: Moist, well-drained, humus-rich
Hardiness: Zone 9
Propagation: Basal or softwood cuttings, in spring
Flowering time: Summer to late autumn

A tender, evergreen subshrub. Foliage aromatic. Flowers red-brown, with purple-tinted calyces, in dense terminal racemes.

- Attracts bees
- Low allergen
- Attracts slugs

Salvia coccinea (Lamiaceae)

Common name: None
Height: 30in (75cm)
Spread: 1ft (30cm)
Aspect: Sun
Soil: Moist, well-drained, humus-rich, fertile
Hardiness: Zone 8
Propagation: Seed in heat in spring
Flowering time: Summer to autumn

A short-lived perennial. Flowers two-lipped, cherry-red, in terminal spikes.

- Attracts bees
- Low allergen
- Attracts slugs
- Short-lived

Salvia farinacea 'Snowball' (Lamiaceae)

Common name: None
Height: 2ft (60cm)
Spread: 1ft (30cm)
Aspect: Sun
Soil: Moist, well-drained, fertile, humus-rich
Hardiness: Zone 9
Propagation: Seed, in heat, in spring
Flowering time: Summer to autumn

A tender perennial, grown usually as an annual. Flowers white, in whorls on tall, slim, dense spikes. Useful bedding plant.

- Attracts bees
- Low allergen
- Attracts slugs

Salvia nemorosa 'Pusztaflamme' A.G.M. (Lamiaceae)

Common name: None
Height: 3ft (90cm)
Spread: 2ft (60cm)
Aspect: Sun
Soil: Moist, well-drained, humus-rich, fertile
Hardiness: Zone 5
Propagation: Basal or softwood cuttings, in spring
Flowering time: Summer to autumn

An upright, hardy perennial. Flowers two-lipped, purple, in dense terminal racemes.

- Attracts bees
- Low allergen
- Attracts slugs

Salvia patens A.G.M.

Salvia patens A.G.M. (Lamiaceae)

Common name: Gentian salvia
Height: 2ft (60cm)
Spread: 18in (45cm)
Aspect: Sun
Soil: Moist, well drained, humus rich, fertile
Hardiness: Zone 8
Propagation: Seed, or division, in spring
Flowering time: midsummer to mid-autumn

A half-hardy, tuberous perennial. Flowers
two-lipped, deep blue, in sparse racemes.

- Attracts bees
- Attracts slugs
- Low allergen

Salvia splendens 'Scarlet King' A.G.M. (Lamiaccae)

Common name: Scarlet sage
Height: 10in (25cm)
Spread 1ft (30cm)
Aspect: Sun
Soil: Moist, well-drained, humus-rich, fertile
Hardiness: Zone 10
Propagation: Sccd in hcat, in carly spring
Flowering time: All summer and autumn

A well-known and much-liked perennial
when it is grown as an annual bedding
plant. Foliage dark green. Flowers scarlet, in
dense terminal spikes.

- Attracts bees
- Attracts slugs
- Low allergen

Salvia splendens 'Sizzler' series (Lamiaceae)

Common name: Scarlet sage
Height: 16in (40cm)
Spread: 14in (35cm)
Aspect: Sun, but not midday
Soil: Moist, well-drained, humus-rich, fertile
Hardiness: Zone 10
Propagation: Seed in heat in early spring
Flowering time: Summer to autumn

A perennial grown invariably as an annual.
This strain has flowers in a wide range of
pastel colors, in dense terminal spikes. It
requires shelter from the sun at its hottest.

- Attracts bees
- Attracts slugs
- Low allergen

Salvia splendens 'Scarlet King' A.G.M.

Salvia splendens 'Sizzler' series

Scabiosa 'Irish Perpetual-flowering' (Dipsacaceae)

Common name: Scabious
Height: 1ft (30cm)
Spread: 18in (45cm)
Aspect: Sun
Soil: Well-drained, fertile
Hardiness: Zone 5
Propagation: Seed in spring
Flowering time: Long periods in summer

A hardy perennial. Flowers solitary, double,
pink, on long stems.

- Good cut flower
- Must not be moved
- Low allergen

Scabiosa 'Irish Perpetual-flowering'

Senecio doronicum

Senecio smithii

Senecio (Asteraceae)
Senecio

A large and very diversified genus of over 1,000 species of annuals, perennials, and shrubs, from an extremely wide range of habitat, and so cultural requirements vary widely; some are very drought-tolerant, others like moist soil. All like full sun. The flowers are daisy-like, and may be solitary or in corymbs. They have a long flowering season. All parts are poisonous, and they are highly allergenic. They are attractive to bees, and make good cut flowers.

Senecio doronicum (Asteraceae)

Common name: None
Height: 16in (40cm)
Spread: 1ft (30cm)
Aspect: Full sun
Soil: Sharply-drained, fertile
Hardiness: Zone 5
Propagation: Division, in spring
Flowering time: Early and midsummer

A hardy perennial. Foliage gray-green, ferny. Flowers single, yellow daisies, in loose corymbs.

- Attracts bees
- Drought-tolerant
- Handsome foliage
- Highly allergenic
- Poisonous

Solanum crispum 'Glasnevin' A.G.M.

Senecio smithii (Asteraceae)

Common name: None
Height: 4ft (1.2m)
Spread: 2ft (60cm)
Aspect: Sun or part shade
Soil: Moist, or wet
Hardiness: Zone 7
Propagation: Division, in spring
Flowering time: Early to late summer

A robust, hardy perennial. Leaves glossy gray-green. Flowers white, with yellow centers, in large corymbs. Bog or aquatic marginal plant.

- Attracts bees
- Good cut flower
- Handsome foliage
- Highly allergenic
- Poisonous

Solanum (Solanaceae)
Solanum

A genus of about 1,500 species, one of which is the potato (S. tuberosum), the other the eggplant (S. melongena). The flowers are five-petalled, shallow cups in white, blue or purple; they are borne singly or in corymbs or cymes, from spring to autumn, followed by fruits. Most are tender, some are half-hardy. They can be evergreen or deciduous.
    They like full sun, and soil which is moist, but well-drained or even sharply-drained. All parts are poisonous, and especially the fruits of some species. (See also under Shrubs.)

Solanum crispum 'Glasnevin' A.G.M. (Solanaceae)

Common name: None
Height: 20ft (6m)
Spread: 3ft (90cm)
Aspect: Sun
Soil: Moist, well-drained, fertile, alkaline
Hardiness: Zone 8
Propagation: Semi-ripe cuttings with bottom heat, in summer
Flowering time: Summer to autumn

An evergreen, or semi-evergreen climber. Flowers fragrant, deep purple-blue, in terminal corymbs.

- Scented flowers
- Poisonous
- Requires space

Sphaeralcea fendleri

Sphaeralcea munroana

Sphaeralcea munroana (Malvaceae)

Common name: None
Height: 32in (80cm)
Spread: 3ft (90cm)
Aspect: Sun
Soil: Sharply-drained
Hardiness: Zone 8
Propagation: Seed in spring; softwood cuttings in summer
Flowering time: Midsummer to mid-autumn

A sprawling perennial. Leaves gray-green. Flowers deep pink, in axillary panicles.

- Drought-tolerant
- Handsome foliage

Stachys byzantina (Lamiaceae)

Common name: Lamb's-ears, Wooly betony
Height: 18in (45cm)
Spread: 2ft (60cm)
Aspect: Sun
Soil: Well-drained, fertile
Hardiness: Zone 5
Propagation: Seed, or division in spring
Flowering time: Early summer to autumn

A mat-forming perennial. Leaves whitish and wooly. Flowers two-lipped, pink-purple, in wooly spikes.

- Attracts bees
- Drought-tolerant
- Good cut flower
- Handsome foliage
- Low allergen
- Attracts slugs
- Divide regularly
- Prone to mildew

Stachys macrantha 'Superba'

Stachys byzantina

Sphaeralcea fendleri (Malvaceae)

Common name: None
Height: 32in (80cm)
Spread: 2ft (60cm)
Aspect: Sun
Soil: Sharply-drained
Hardiness: Zone 8
Propagation: Seed in spring; softwood cuttings in summer
Flowering time: Early summer to mid-autumn

A woody, sprawling subshrub. Leaves gray-green. Flowers pale pink, in axillary panicles.

- Drought-tolerant
- Handsome foliage
- Short-lived

Stachys macrantha 'Superba' (Lamiaceae)

Common name: None
Height: 2ft (60cm)
Spread: 1ft (30cm)
Aspect: Sun or part shade
Soil: Well-drained, fertile
Hardiness: Zone 5
Propagation: Seed or division, in spring
Flowering time: Early summer to autumn

An upright perennial. Flowers two-lipped, hooded, purple, in dense spikes.

- Attracts bees
- Good cut flower
- Low allergen
- Attracts slugs
- Prone to mildew
- Requires staking

Stachys officinalis 'Rosea Superba'

Streptocarpus hybridus

Streptocarpus 'Crystal Ice'

Stachys officinalis 'Rosea Superba' (Lamiaceae)

Common name: Common betony
Height: 2ft (60cm)
Spread: 1ft (30cm)
Aspect: Sun or part shade
Soil: Well-drained, fertile
Hardiness: Zone 5
Propagation: Division, in spring
Flowering time: Early summer to autumn

A dwarf perennial with basal leaf rosettes.
Flowers two-lipped, rose-pink, in upright,
dense spikes.

- Attracts bees
- Drought-tolerant
- Good cut flower
- Attracts slugs
- Prone to mildew

Streptocarpus hybridus (Gesneriaceae)

Common name: None
Height: 1ft (30cm)
Spread: 18in (45cm)
Aspect: Part shade
Soil: Moist, humus-rich, well-drained; just
damp in winter
Hardiness: Zone 10
Propagation: Division, or leaf cuttings, in
spring/summer
Flowering time: Spring to autumn; all year
in warm areas

Leaves hairy, wrinkled, veined. Flowers
tubular, in a wide range of colors, in cymes.

- Handsome foliage

Streptocarpus 'Crystal Ice' (Gesneriaceae)

Common name: None
Height: 1ft (30cm)
Spread: 1ft (30cm)
Aspect: Part shade
Soil: Moist, well-drained, humus-rich; just
damp in winter
Hardiness: Zone 10
Propagation: Division, or leaf cuttings, in
spring/summer
Flowering time: All year round

Leaves in rosettes, hairy, veined. Flowers
tubular, white, with lilac throats, in cymes.

- Handsome foliage

Symphytum x *uplandicum* (Boraginaceae)

Common name: None
Height: 6ft (1.8m)
Spread: 4ft (1.2m)
Aspect: Sun or part shade
Soil: Moist, fertile
Hardiness: Zone 5
Propagation: Seed or division, in spring;
division in autumn
Flowering time: Late spring to late summer

A large much-branched, rhizomatous,
invasive perennial. Flowers purple-blue from
pinkish buds, in cymes.

- Low allergen
- Invasive
- Poisonous
- Requires space
- Skin irritant

Symphytum x *uplandicum*

Thunbergia alata (Acanthaceae)

Common name: Clockvine
Height: 8ft (2.5m)
Spread: 2ft (60cm)
Aspect: Sun
Soil: Moist, well-drained, fertile
Hardiness: Zone 10
Propagation: Seed in heat, or layer, in spring; greenwood cuttings in early summer
Flowering time: From summer to autumn

An evergreen, perennial climber, grown often as an annual. Flowers single salvers, orange or yellow, with chocolate-colored centers.

● Evergreen

Thunbergia alata

Tiarella wherryi A.G.M.

Tiarella wherryi A.G.M. (Saxifragaceae)

Common name: None
Height: 8in (20cm)
Spread: 6in (15cm)
Aspect: Part or full shade
Soil: Moist, humus-rich,
Hardiness: Zone 6
Propagation: Seed when ripe; seed, or division, in spring
Flowering time: Late spring to early summer

Slow-growing, compact, woodland perennial. Flowers white, tinged pink, in racemes.

● Low allergen ● Attracts slugs

Tradescantia x *andersoniana* 'Isis' A.G.M.

Tradescantia x andersoniana 'Isis' A.G.M. (Commelinaceae)

Common name: None
Height: 2ft (60cm)
Spread: 2ft (60cm)
Aspect: Sun or part shade
Soil: Moist, fertile
Hardiness: Zone 5
Propagation: Division, in spring or autumn
Flowering time: Early summer to autumn

A clump-forming perennial. Flowers three-petaled, flat, dark blue, in paired terminal cymes.

● Low allergen ● Divide regularly
● Skin irritant

Tradescantia x andersoniana 'Osprey' A.G.M. (Commelinaceae)

Common name: None
Height: 2ft (60cm)
Spread: 2ft (60cm)
Aspect: Sun or part shade
Soil: Moist, fertile
Hardiness: Zone 5
Propagation: Division, in spring or autumn
Flowering time: Early summer to autumn

A clump forming perennial. Flowers three-petaled, flat, white, in paired terminal cymes.

● Low allergen ● Divide regularly
● Skin irritant

Tradescantia x *andersoniana* 'Osprey' A.G.M.

TROPAEOLUM (Tropaeolaceae)
Nasturtium

A genus of just under 100 species of mostly tuberous perennials and climbing, trailing, or bushy annuals. Nasturtiums have edible leaves and come from cool mountain regions. The flowers are trumpet-shaped, with five clawed petals, borne singly over long periods in summer and autumn.

Nasturtiums like full sun and moist, but well-drained soil. They can self-seed freely, and are prone to attack by slugs and blackfly. The climbing varieties require support, or will scramble up through other plants.

Tropaeolum polyphyllum

Verbascum 'Helen Johnson' A.G.M.

Tropaeolum polyphyllum
(Tropaeolaceae)

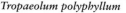

Common name: Wreath nasturtium
Height: 4in (10cm)
Spread: Indefinite
Aspect: Sun
Soil: Well-drained, humus-rich
Hardiness: Zone 8
Propagation: Division in early spring; stem or basal cuttings in summer
Flowering time: Long period in summer

A tuberous, trailing herbaceous perennial. Leaves glaucous, blue-green. Flowers yellow. Can travel underground for long distances.

- Handsome foliage
- Attracts slugs

Tropaeolum speciosum A.G.M.
(Tropaeolaceae)

Common name: Vermilion nasturtium
Height: 10ft (3m)
Spread: Indefinite
Aspect: Sun, roots in cool shade
Soil: Acid, moist, humus-rich,
Hardiness: Zone 8
Propagation: Division, in early spring
Flowering time: Summer to autumn

A frail perennial climber. Leaves 5- and 7-palmate, green. Flowers bright red, spurred, with clawed petals. Never reappears where it was planted, but several feet away, so tread carefully.

- Handsome foliage
- Invasive

Tropaeolum speciosum A.G.M.

Verbascum 'Helen Johnson' A.G.M.
(Scrophulariaceae)

Common name: None
Height: 3ft (90cm)
Spread: 18in (45cm)
Aspect: Sun
Soil: Poor, sharply-drained
Hardiness: Zone 7
Propagation: Division, in spring; root cuttings in winter
Flowering time: Early to late summer

An evergreen perennial. Leaves downy, gray-green. Flowers pinkish-brown saucers, in erect branched spikes.

- Attracts bees
- Prone to mildew
- Drought-tolerant
- Seeds everywhere
- Evergreen
- Handsome foliage

VERBENA (Verbenaceae)
Verbena

A genus of about 250 species of subshrubs, annuals, and perennials; many of the last group are grown widely as annuals.

They grow in both tropical and temperate zones, and in moist or dry but open, sunny sites. The flowers are salveriform, and in cymes, panicles, or racemes; they are borne over a long period in summer.

Verbenas like humus-rich, well-drained soil, and full sun. They are very attractive to butterflies. They are prone to attack by slugs, and powdery mildew.

Verbena bonariensis (Verbenaceae)

Common name: None
Height: 6ft (1.8m)
Spread: 30in (75cm)
Aspect: Sun
Soil: Well-drained, fertile
Hardiness: Zone 8
Propagation: Seed or division, in spring
Flowering time: Midsummer to early autumn

A clump-forming perennial. Flowers lilac, salverform, in cymes. Loved by butterflies.

- Attracts butterflies
- Prone to mildew
- Drought-tolerant
- Seeds everywhere

Verbena bonariensis

Verbena hastata

Verbena x *hybrida* 'Peaches and Cream'

Verbena x *hybrida* 'Loveliness'

Verbena hastata (Verbenaceae)

Common name: None
Height: 4ft (1.2m)
Spread: 2ft (60cm)
Aspect: Sun
Soil: Well-drained, fertile
Hardiness: Zone 3
Propagation: Seed or division, in spring
Flowering time: Early summer to autumn

An upright perennial. Flowers white, pink-purple, or violet-blue, in stiff panicles.

- Attracts butterflies
- Good cut flower
- Attracts slugs
- Prone to mildew

Verbena x *hybrida* 'Red Cascade'

Verbena x hybrida 'Loveliness' (Verbenaceae)

Common name: None
Height: 18in (45cm)
Spread: 20in (50cm)
Aspect: Sun
Soil: Humus-rich, well-drained
Hardiness: Zone 9
Propagation: Division in spring; stem-tip cuttings in late summer
Flowering time: Summer and autumn

A tender perennial grown almost invariably as an annual. Flowers salverform, pink, in corymb-like panicles.

- Attracts butterflies
- Attracts slugs
- Prone to mildew

Verbena x hybrida 'Peaches and Cream' (Verbenaceae)

Common name: None
Height: 18in (45cm)
Spread: 20in (50cm)
Aspect: Sun
Soil: Well-drained, humus-rich
Hardiness: Zone 9
Propagation: Division in spring; stem-tip cuttings in late summer
Flowering time: Summer and autumn

A tender perennial, grown usually as an annual. Flowers salverform, orange-pink, fading to apricot and then cream, in panicles.

- Attracts butterflies
- Attracts slugs
- Prone to mildew

Verbena x hybrida 'Red Cascade' (Verbenaceae)

Common name: None
Height: 18in (45cm)
Spread: 20in (50cm)
Aspect: Sun
Soil: Well-drained, humus-rich
Hardiness: Zone 9
Propagation: Division, in spring; stem-tip cuttings in late summer
Flowering time: Summer and autumn

A tender perennial grown almost invariably as an annual. Flowers salverform, scarlet, in panicles.

- Atteacts bees
- Attracts slugs
- Prone to mildew

Veronica spicata ssp. *incana*
(Scrophulariaceae)

Common name: Wooly speedwell
Height: 1ft (30cm)
Spread: 1ft (30cm)
Aspect: Sun or part shade
Soil: Moist, well-drained, humus-rich, fertile
Hardiness: Zone 3
Propagation: Seed or division, in autumn; division in spring
Flowering time: Early to late summer

Mat-forming. Leaves silver, hairy. Flowers star-shaped, blue, in dense terminal racemes.

- Attracts bees
- Handsome foliage
- Low allergen
- Prone to mildew

Veronica spicata 'Rotfuchs'
(Scrophulariaceae)

Common name: None
Height: 1ft (30cm)
Spread: 1ft (30cm)
Aspect: Sun or part shade
Soil: Moist, well-drained, humus-rich, fertile
Hardiness: Zone 3
Propagation: Division, in spring or autumn; seed in autumn
Flowering time: Early to late summer

A mat-forming perennial. Flowers deep pink, star-shaped, in dense terminal racemes.

- Attracts bees
- Low allergen
- Prone to mildew

Viola 'Columbine' (Violaceae)

Common name: None
Height: 8in (20cm)
Spread: 1ft (30cm)
Aspect: Sun or part shade
Soil: Moist, well-drained, humus-rich, fertile
Hardiness: Zone 7
Propagation: Division, or stem-tip cuttings, in spring
Flowering time: Spring and summer

An evergreen, short-lived perennial. Flowers lilac and white, streaked purple.

- Evergreen
- Good cut flower
- Low allergen
- Scented flowers
- Attracts slugs
- Must deadhead
- Prone to mildew
- Short-lived

Viola cornuta 'Alba' A.G.M. (Violaceae)

Common name: None
Height: 6in (15cm)
Spread: 18in (45cm)
Aspect: Sun or part shade
Soil: Moist, humus-rich, fertile
Hardiness: Zone 7
Propagation: Seed when ripe, or in spring
Flowering time: Spring to summer

A short-lived, evergreen, rhizomatous perennial. Flowers scented, white; flowers again later if sheared over.

- Evergreen
- Low allergen
- Scented flowers
- Attracts slugs
- Must deadhead
- Prone to mildew
- Short-lived

Veronica spicata ssp. *incana*

Veronica spicata 'Rotfuchs'

Viola 'Columbine'

Viola cornuta 'Alba' A.G.M.

Viola 'Etain'

Viola 'Jackanapes' A.G.M.

Zauschneria californica A.G.M.

Zephyranthes candida

Viola 'Etain' (Violaceae)

Common name: None
Height: 8in (20cm)
Spread: 1ft (30cm)
Aspect: Sun or part shade
Soil: Moist, well-drained, humus-rich, fertile
Hardiness: Zone 7
Propagation: Division, or stem-tip cuttings, in spring
Flowering time: Spring and summer

A short-lived, evergreen perennial. Flowers cream, margined lilac, with orange centers.

- Evergreen
- Low allergen
- Attracts slugs
- Must deadhead
- Prone to mildew
- Short-lived

Viola 'Jackanapes' A.G.M. (Violaceae)

Common name: None
Height: 8in (20cm)
Spread: 1ft (30cm)
Aspect: Sun or part shade
Soil: Moist, well-drained, humus-rich
Hardiness: Zone 7
Propagation: Division, or stem-tip cuttings, in spring
Flowering time: Spring to summer

A short-lived, evergreen perennial. Flowers have chocolate-colored upper petals, and yellow, streaked purple, lower ones. Deadheading prolongs flowering.

- Evergreen
- Low allergen
- Attracts slugs
- Must deadhead
- Prone to mildew
- Short-lived

Zauschneria californica A.G.M. (Onagraceae)

Common name: None
Height: 1ft (30cm)
Spread: 20in (50cm)
Aspect: Sun
Soil: Well-drained
Hardiness: Zone 8
Propagation: Seed or basal cuttings in spring
Flowering time: Late spring and early summer

A rhizomatous, evergreen perennial. Leaves gray-green. Flowers tubular, scarlet, in racemes.

- Evergreen
- Handsome foliage
- Attracts slugs

Zephyranthes candida (Amaryllidaceae)

Common name: None
Height: 8in (20cm)
Spread: 3in (8cm)
Aspect: Sun; no winter wet
Soil: Moist, well-drained
Hardiness: Zone 9
Propagation: Seed in warmth when ripe; offsets in spring
Flowering time: Summer to early autumn

A bulbous perennial. Flowers crocus-like, solitary, white. A trouble-free plant.

SHRUBS

※

Shrubs are woody plants that usually have more than one stem arising at or near the ground, and they seldom reach more than 20ft (6m) in height; they differ from trees which normally have only one stem and can grow to considerable heights. Subshrubs either have stems that are woody only at the base, such as *Perovskias*, or have stems like *Fuchsias* that die back to some extent over winter. Subshrubs are often cultivated alongside perennials in mixed borders and given similar treatment. Both shrubs and subshrubs are generally long-lived, given correct conditions, and are easy to cultivate, requiring little attention.

Like perennials, shrubs can be evergreen or deciduous, and some of the latter have stunning autumn displays. Again, they vary widely in their degree of hardiness and the reader is advised to refer to the section on hardiness before buying. In cold climates, one can grown smaller, tender shrubs in containers and bring them indoors over winter; this is not possible with the larger varieties, which may be kept indoors all year round. Because the growth is above ground, it is obviously not effective to surface-mulch tender shrubs, but covering the plant with fleece or bubble polythene to insulate against the cold can help.

Certain shrubs are not suited to the small garden because of their height and spread; smaller shrubs and subshrubs which will not overwhelm neighboring perennials can be grown in mixed borders. As a general rule, shrubs do not tend to have a very long flowering season, but there are some notable exceptions such as *Abelia* and *Abutilon*. Shrubs also have very different pruning requirements: some have to be pruned because they flower only on the growth of the previous season, and others for shape and size. The text highlights those plants unsuitable for small gardens and gives information on pruning. As with perennials, some shrubs require acid soil conditions, and again these are indicated in the text. Good drainage is equally essential for shrubs as for perennials.

Abelia x grandiflora A.G.M.
(Caprifoliaceae)

Common name: Glossy abelia
Height: 10ft (3m)
Spread: 12ft (4m)
Aspect: Sun
Soil: Fertile, well-drained
Hardiness: Zone 5
Propagation: Semi-ripe cuttings in late summer
Flowering time: Midsummer to autumn

A semi-evergreen or evergreen shrub. Leaves ovate, glossy green. Flowers in terminal panicles and axillary cymes, fragrant, funnel-shaped, white tinted pink. Prune in early spring only to remove wayward shoots.

- Evergreen
- Requires space
- Scented flowers

Abelia schumannii (Caprifoliaceae)

Common name: None
Height: 6ft (1.8m)
Spread: 10ft (3m)
Aspect: Sun
Soil: Well-drained, fertile
Hardiness: Zone 6
Propagation: Semi-ripe cuttings in late summer
Flowering time: Late summer through autumn

A deciduous, arching shrub. Leaves ovate, bronze, turning green. Flowers lilac-pink funnels, orange markings, in axillary cymes. Prune in early spring to remove wayward shoots.

- Scented flowers
- Requires space

ABUTILON (Malvaceae)
Flowering-maple

A genus of some 150 species, from subtropical and tropical regions of all five continents. They vary in their degree of hardiness, and most are Zone 8 or 9, but *A. theophrastii* is Zone 4. They may be evergreen or deciduous, and shrubs or trees: only the shrubs are featured here.

There are large numbers of hybrids. The flowers are bell-shaped, usually pendent, come in all colors, and are borne for long periods from spring to autumn. They vary in their pruning requirements, and each plant covered is given a regime.

They make excellent conservatory plants in colder regions.

Abutilon 'Ashford Red' A.G.M. (Malvaceae)

Common name: None
Height: 10ft (3m)
Spread: 10ft (3m)
Aspect: Sun
Soil: Well-drained, fertile
Hardiness: Zone 8
Propagation: Greenwood cuttings in summer
Flowering time: Spring to autumn

An erect or spreading evergreen shrub. Leaves ovate/rounded, mid-green. Flowers pendent or nodding, cup-shaped, red. Prune only lightly in summer.

- Evergreen
- Requires staking

Abutilon 'Boule de Neige' (Malvaceae)

Common name: None
Height: 12ft (4m)
Spread: 10ft (3m)
Aspect: Sun
Soil: Well-drained, fertile
Hardiness Zone 8
Propagation: Greenwood cuttings in summer
Flowering time: All summer

An evergreen shrub. Leaves ovate. Flowers white, pendent. Prune lightly in spring.

- Evergreen

Abutilon 'Boule de Neige'

Abelia x grandiflora A.G.M.

Abelia schumannii

Abutilon 'Ashford Red' A.G.M.

Abutilon 'Canary Bird' A.G.M.

Abutilon 'Kentish Belle' A.G.M.

Abutilon 'Cannington Peter' A.G.M.

Abutilon 'Cannington Peter' A.G.M. (Malvaceae)

Common name: None
Height: 6ft (1.8m)
Spread: 3ft (90cm)
Aspect: Sun
Soil: Well-drained, fertile
Hardiness: Zone 8
Propagation: Greenwood cuttings in summer
Flowering time: All summer

Leaves ovate/rounded, variegated yellow. Flowers deep maroon, bell-shaped, pendent. Very desirable. Prune only lightly in spring.

● Handsome foliage ● Short-lived

Abutilon 'Kentish Belle' A.G.M. (Malvaceae)

Common name: None
Height: 8ft (2.5m)
Spread: 6ft (1.8m)
Aspect: Sun
Soil: Fertile, well-drained
Hardiness: Zone 8
Propagation: Greenwood cuttings in summer
Flowering time: All summer and autumn

A tall, but extremely elegant, semi evergreen shrub. Stems arching, with rows of pendent flowers, with yellow petals protruding from red calyces. Prune only lightly in spring to preserve shape.

● Requires staking

Abutilon 'Canary Bird' A.G.M. (Malvaceae)

Common name: None
Height: 10ft (3m)
Spread: 10ft (3m)
Aspect: Sun
Soil: Well-drained, fertile
Hardiness: Zone 8
Propagation: Greenwood cuttings in summer
Flowering time: Spring to autumn

A vigorous, hybrid, evergreen shrub. Leaves ovate/rounded, mid-green. Flowers bell-shaped, pendent, yellow. Prune only lightly in spring to preserve shape.

● Requires staking

Allamanda cathartica

Allamanda cathartica (Apocynaceae)

Common name: None
Height: 52ft (16m)
Spread: 6ft (1.8m)
Aspect: Full sun
Soil: Moist, fertile
Hardiness: Zone 11
Propagation: Seed in heat in spring; greenwood cuttings, in spring-summer
Flowering time: Summer to autumn

A very large, evergreen, climbing shrub. Flowers in axillary and terminal cymes, trumpet-shaped, yellow. Prune to fit available space, in spring or after flowering.

● Evergreen ● Poisonous
　　　　　　　● Requires space
　　　　　　　● Skin irritant

Anisodontea capensis

Antirrhinum sempervirens

Argyranthemum frutescens

Anisodontea capensis (Malvaceae)

Common name: None
Height: 3ft (90cm)
Spread: 32in (80cm)
Aspect: Full sun
Soil: Well-drained, fertile
Hardiness: Zone 9
Propagation: Seed in warmth in spring; semi-ripe cuttings in summer
Flowering time: Spring to autumn

A woody, evergreen, South African shrub. Leaves ovate/triangular, shallowly lobed, mid-green. Flowers solitary or in racemes of 2 or 3, cup-shaped, pale pink with a darker center. Prune lightly, only to preserve shape.

- Evergreen
- Drought-tolerant

Antirrhinum sempervirens (Scrophulariaceae)

Common name: None
Height: 8in (20cm)
Spread: 1ft (30cm)
Aspect: Full sun
Soil: Well-drained, fertile
Hardiness: Zone 7
Propagation: Seed in spring or autumn; softwood cuttings in summer
Flowering time: Early and midsummer

A dwarf, decumbent shrub. Leaves oblong/ovate, sticky-hairy, mid-green. Flowers white, with yellow palates and purple veins, from the leaf axils. *A. pulverulentum* (Zone 9) is similar, with yellow flowers.

- Good cut flower
- Low allergen
- Must deadhead
- Prone to mildew
- Seeds everywhere
- Short-lived

ARGYRANTHEMUM (Asteraceae)
Argyranthemum

A genus of some 25 species of evergreen subshrubs from a wide range of habitats in Madeira and the Canary Islands. There are many hybrids in cultivation. The evergreen, pinnatisect foliage may be green or glaucous. The daisy-like flowers are solitary or in corymbs, and may be single, double, or anemone-centered. The flowering season is from late spring to early autumn, and they make excellent bedding plants. They are available in a range of colors from white, through yellow to pink. All are highly allergenic. Deadheading improves the length of flowering time.

Argyranthemum frutescens (Asteraceae)

Common name: Marguerite
Height: 28in (70cm)
Spread: 28in (70cm)
Aspect: Full sun
Soil: Well-drained
Hardiness: Zone 9
Propagation: Seed, in heat, in spring
Flowering time: All summer

A species subshrub, not grown very often because of the plethora of superior hybrids. Leaves pinnatisect, green. Flowers single, white, with a yellow disc, borne profusely. Prune after flowering to within 1in (2.5cm) of previous year's growth .

- Evergreen
- Good cut flower
- Highly allergenic
- Must deadhead

Argyranthemum 'Jamaica Primrose' A.G.M. (Asteraceae)

Common name: None
Height: 42in (1m)
Spread: 3ft (90cm)
Aspect: Full sun
Soil: Well-drained
Hardiness: Zone 9
Propagation: Greenwood cuttings in spring
Flowering time: All summer and autumn

A very handsome hybrid. Leaves pinnatisect, toothed, gray-green. Flowers solitary, single, yellow with a darker disc. A lovely standard plant. Prune after flowering to within 1in (2.5cm) of previous year's growth.

- Evergreen
- Good cut flower
- Highly allergenic
- Must deadhead

Argyranthemum 'Jamaica Primrose' A.G.M.

Argyranthemum 'Petite Pink' A.G.M.

Argyranthemum 'Sugar Button'

Argyranthemum 'Summer Stars'

Bomarea caldasii A.G.M.

Argyranthemum 'Petite Pink' A.G.M.
(Asteraceae)

Common name: None
Height: 1ft (30cm)
Spread: 1ft (30cm)
Aspect: Full sun
Soil: Well-drained
Hardiness: Zone 9
Propagation: Greenwood cuttings in spring;
semi-ripe cuttings in summer
Flowering time: All summer

A compact, rounded, hybrid subshrub.
Leaves pinnatisect, gray-green. Flowers
solitary, single, pale pink, with yellow discs.
Prune after flowering by cutting back to
within 1in (2.5cm) of previous year's
growth.

● Evergreen ● Highly allergenic
● Good cut flower   Must deadhead

Argyranthemum 'Sugar Button'
(Asteraceae)

Common name: None
Height: 18in (45cm)
Spread: 18in (45cm)
Aspect: Full sun
Soil: Well-drained
Hardiness: Zone 9
Propagation: Greenwood cuttings in spring;
semi-ripe cuttings in summer
Flowering time: All summer

A recent hybrid. Leaves pinnatisect, gray-
green. Flowers solitary, double, white,
with yellow discs. Prune after flowering by
cutting back to within 1in (2.5cm) of
previous year's growth.

● Evergreen ● Highly allergenic
● Good cut flower ● Must deadhead

Argyranthemum 'Summer Stars'
(Asteraceae)

Common name: None
Height: 16in (40cm)
Spread: 16in (40cm)
Aspect: Full sun
Soil: Well-drained
Hardiness: Zone 9
Propagation: Greenwood cuttings in spring;
semi-ripe cuttings in summer
Flowering time: All summer

Another recent clone. Leaves pinnatisect,
toothed, gray-green. Flowers solitary,
single, pale pink with deep pink basal
regions, and yellow disc florets. Prune after
flowering by cutting back to within 1in
(2.5cm) of previous year's growth.

● Evergreen ● Highly allergenic
● Good cut flower ● Must deadhead

*List of other Argyranthemum cultivars
given an Award of Garden merit
(all Zone 9)*

'Cornish Gold'
'Donington Hero'
Gracile 'Chelsea Girl'
'Levada Cream'
'Mary Cheek'
'Quinta White'
'Snowstorm'
'Vancouver'
'Whiteknights'

Bomarea caldasii A.G.M.
(Alstroemeriaceae)

Common name: None
Height: 12ft (4m)
Spread: 3ft (90cm)
Aspect: Full sun
Soil: Moist, well-drained
Hardiness: Zone 9
Propagation: Seed in heat in spring; division
in late winter or early spring
Flowering time: Late spring to autumn

A deciduous, twining, climbing shrub.
Leaves oblong, mid-green. Inflorescence in
spherical umbels of as many as 40, narrow,
tubular, orange or brick-red flowers,
spotted inside. Prune flowered shoots to the
ground in autumn.

● Requires space

Bougainvillea glabra A.G.M. (Nyctaginaceae)

Common name: None
Height: 25ft (7.6m)
Spread: 6ft (1.8m)
Aspect: Full sun
Soil: Well-drained, fertile
Hardiness: Zone 9
Propagation: Softwood cuttings in spring; semi-ripe cuttings in summer; layer in autumn
Flowering time: Summer to autumn

A large, evergreen climber. Flowers very small, white, insignificant. Bracts of white or magenta, in large clusters. Prune in early spring by cutting back side shoots to within 3–4 buds of permanent framework.

- Drought-tolerant
- Evergreen
- Requires space

Brachyglottis Dunedin group 'Sunshine' (Asteraceae)

Common name: None
Height: 5ft (1.5m)
Spread: 6ft (1.8m) or more
Aspect: Full sun
Soil: Well-drained
Hardiness: Zone 5
Propagation: Semi-ripe cuttings in summer
Flowering time: Summer to autumn

An evergreen hybrid of garden origin. Leaves elliptic, gray-hairy. Flowers in loose terminal panicles, daisy-like, pale yellow, with darker yellow discs. Good for coastal sites. Prune after flowering by deadheading, and removing shoots which spoil symmetry.

- Attracts bees
- Evergreen
- Handsome foliage
- Requires space

Brugmansia sanguinea A.G.M. (Solanaceae)

Common name: None
Height: 30ft (9m)
Spread: 10ft (3m)
Aspect: Full sun
Soil: Sharply- drained, fertile
Hardiness: Zone 9
Propagation: Seed in heat in spring
Flowering time: Late spring to autumn

A highly toxic, very large shrub. Leaves large, ovate, wavy-edged, mid-green. Flowers tubular pendent orange/yellow trumpets, up to 10in (25cm) long. Deadhead and remove shoots which spoil symmetry after flowering.

- Poisonous
- Requires space

Bupleurum fruticosum (Apiaceae)

Common name: Shrubby hare's ear
Height: 6ft (1.8m)
Spread: 8ft (2.5m)
Aspect: Full sun
Soil: Well-drained
Hardiness: Zone 7
Propagation: Seed in spring
Flowering time: Midsummer to autumn

An evergreen, spreading shrub. Leaves narrow, obovate, blue-green. Flowers small, yellow stars, but borne in a large, domed, terminal umbel. Prune in spring to maintain symmetry; deadhead regularly.

- Attracts bees
- Drought-tolerant
- Evergreen
- Requires space
- Seeds everywhere

Bougainvillea glabra A.G.M.

Brachyglottis Dunedin group 'Sunshine'

Brugmansia sanguinea A.G.M.

Bupleurum fruticosum

Caesalpinia pulcherrima

Calluna vulgaris 'County Wicklow' A.G.M.

Calluna vulgaris 'Kinlochruel' A.G.M.

Calceolaria integrifolia A.G.M.

Caesalpinia pulcherrima (Caesalpiniaceae)

Common name: None
Height: 20ft (6m)
Spread: 16ft (5m)
Aspect: Sun
Soil: Moist, well-drained, fertile
Hardiness: Zone 9
Propagation: Soaked seed in heat in spring
Flowering time: Spring to autumn

A large, evergreen shrub. Leaves pinnate. Flowers bowl-shaped, in erect racemes of up to 40, yellow or orange-yellow, with red sepals and stamens. Prune by deadheading, and cutting out shoots to preserve symmetry.

● Evergreen   ● Requires space

Calceolaria integrifolia A.G.M.
(Scrophulariaceae)

Common name: Slipper flower, Slipperwort
Height: 3ft (90cm)
Spread: 1ft (30cm)
Aspect: Sun or half shade
Soil: Acid, gritty, fertile
Hardiness: Zone 9
Propagation: Seed or division, in spring
Flowering time: All summer

A lax, evergreen subshrub. Leaves ovate/lance, toothed, gray-green. Flowers yellow, in cymes of up to 35. Best treated as an annual in cold areas.

● Evergreen   ● Attracts slugs

Calluna vulgaris 'County Wicklow' A.G.M.
(Ericaceae)

Common name: Heather
Height: 10in (25cm)
Spread: 14in (35cm)
Aspect: Full sun
Soil: Acid, well-drained, humus-rich
Hardiness: Zone 4
Propagation: Layer in spring; semi-ripe cuttings in summer
Flowering time: Midsummer to autumn

A prostrate, compact cultivar. Flowers large, double, pale pink, in lengthy racemes. Prune after flowering to within 1in (2.5cm) of previous year's growth.

● Evergreen

Calluna vulgaris 'Kinlochruel' A.G.M.
(Ericaceae)

Common name: Heather
Height: 10in (25cm)
Spread: 16in (40cm)
Aspect: Full sun
Soil: Acid, well-drained, humus-rich
Hardiness: Zone 4
Propagation: Layer in spring; semi-ripe cuttings in summer
Flowering time: Midsummer to autumn

A handsome clone with leaves of bright green, which turn bronze in winter. Flowers white, double, in long racemes. Prune after flowering to within 1in (2.5cm) of previous year's growth.

● Evergreen

Calluna vulgaris 'Spring Torch' (Ericaceae)

Common name: Heather
Height: 16in (40cm)
Spread: 30in (75cm)
Aspect: Full sun
Soil: Acid, humus-rich, well-drained
Hardiness: Zone 4
Propagation: Layer in spring; semi-ripe
cuttings in summer
Flowering time: Midsummer to late autumn

A clone with mid-green, hairless leaves,
orange in winter. Flowers bell-shaped, in
racemes, mauve-pink. Prune after flowering
to within 1in (2.5cm) of previous year's
growth.

● Evergreen

Calluna vulgaris 'Spring Torch'

*List of other Calluna vulgaris cultivars
awarded the A.G.M. of the R.H.S
All Zone 4.*

'Allegro'
'Annemarie'
'Anthony Davis'
'Battle of Arnhem'
'Beoley Gold'
'Dark Star'
'Darkness'
'Elsie Purnell'
'Finale'
'Firefly'
'Gold Haze'
'J.H. Hamilton'
'Jimmy Dyce'
'Joy Vanstone'
'Mair's Variety'
'Mullion'
'Orange Queen'
'Radnor'
'Red Star'
'Robert Chapman'
'Roland Haagen'
'Serlei Aurea'
'Silver Queen'
'Silver Rose'
'Sir John Charrington'
'Sister Anne'
'Spring Cream'
'Sunset'
'Underwoodii'
'White Lawn'
'Wickwar Flame'

Campsis grandiflora (Bignoniaceae)

Common name: Trumpetvine
Height: 30ft (9m)
Spread: 5ft (1.5m)
Aspect: Part shade
Soil: Moist, well-drained
Hardiness: Zone 7
Propagation: Seed in autumn; semi-ripe
cuttings in summer
Flowering time: Late summer to autumn

A robust, deciduous shrub. Flowers open
funnels, red, in pendent panicles. Prune side
shoots in late winter/early spring to within
3–4 buds of permanent framework.

● Prone to mildew
● Requires space
● Requires staking

Ceanothus 'Skylark' (Rhamnaceae)

Common name: None
Height: 6ft (1.8m)
Spread: 5ft (1.5m)
Aspect: Full sun
Soil: Well-drained, fertile
Hardiness: Zone 8
Propagation: Semi-ripe cuttings in summer
Flowering time: Late spring to early summer

An evergreen, compact, profuse-flowering
shrub. Leaves oblong, toothed, glossy-green.
Flowers in lateral and terminal panicles,
dark blue. Prune to preserve symmetry and
to deadhead.

● Evergreen   ● Highly allergenic
                ● Requires space

Ceanothus thyrsiflorus repens A.G.M.
(Rhamnaceae)

Common name: Blue blossom ceanothus
Height: 3ft (90cm)
Spread: 8ft (2.5m)
Aspect: Full sun
Soil: Well-drained, fertile
Hardiness: Zone 8
Propagation: Semi-ripe cuttings in summer
Flowering time: Late spring to early summer

An evergreen, sprawling, free-flowering
shrub. Leaves ovate, toothed, glossy-green.
Flowers in lateral and terminal panicles,
pale blue. Prune to preserve shape.

● Evergreen   ● Highly allergenic
                ● Requires space

Campsis grandiflora

Ceanothus 'Skylark'

Ceanothus thyrsiflorus repens A.G.M.

Cestrum parqui A.G.M. (Solanaceae)

Common name: Chilean cestrum
Height: 6ft (1.8m)
Spread: 6ft (1.8m)
Aspect: Sun or half shade
Soil: Well-drained, fertile
Hardiness: Zone 8
Propagation: Softwood cuttings in summer
Flowering time: Summer to autumn

A deciduous, upright shrub from Chile. Leaves linerar/lance, mid-green. Flowers greenish-yellow, tubular, scented, in large axillary and terminal cymes, followed by brown berries. Prune annually, in spring, hard back to near the base.

● Scented flowers

Choisya 'Aztec Pearl' A.G.M. (Rutaceae)

Common name: None
Height: 8ft (2.5m)
Spread: 8ft (2.5m)
Aspect: Full sun
Soil: Well-drained, fertile
Hardiness: Zone 7
Propagation: Semi-ripe cuttings in summer
Flowering time: Late spring; late summer and autumn

An evergreen shrub. Leaves aromatic. Flowers white, tinged pink, scented, in axillary cymes. Prune by deadheading and cutting out shoots which spoil symmetry.

● Aromatic foliage
● Evergreen
● Scented flowers
● Attracts slugs
● Requires space

Choisya ternata A.G.M. (Rutaceae)

Common name: Mexican-orange
Height: 8ft (2.5m)
Spread: 8ft (2.5m)
Aspect: Full sun
Soil: Fertile, well-drained
Hardiness: Zone 7
Propagation: Semi-ripe cuttings in summer
Flowering time: Late spring; late summer and autumn

An evergreen shrub. Leaves aromatic. Scented flowers, white, in axillary corymbs. Deadheading and removal of wayward shoots is all the pruning required.

● Aromatic foliage
● Evergreen
● Scented flowers
● Attracts slugs
● Requires space

CISTUS (Cistaceae)
Cistus

A genus of some 20 evergreen shrubs from stony or rocky areas in S. Europe, N. Africa, the Canaries and Turkey. They have, like Day lilies, flowers which last only one day, but which appear in succession over a long period from early to late summer. They can sometimes be short-lived. They should be grown in open, gritty soil in full sun. Prune to preserve symmetry, and deadhead, annually after flowering. They do not recover from being cut hard back, and old plants should be replaced.

Cistus x *dansereaui* (Cistaceae)

Common name: None
Height: 3ft (90cm)
Spread: 3ft (90cm)
Aspect: Full sun
Soil: Well-drained
Hardiness: Zone 8
Propagation: Seed as soon as ripe; softwood cuttings in summer
Flowering time: All summer

An upright shrub. Leaves lance-shaped, dark green. Flowers in terminal cymes, white, with crimson marks at the base of petals. Prune by deadheading and to preserve symmetry.

● Evergreen
● Drought-tolerant
● Short-lived

Cestrum parqui A.G.M.

Choisya 'Aztec Pearl' A.G.M.

Choisya ternata A.G.M.

Cistus x *dansereaui*

Cistus 'Elma' A.G.M

Cistus ladanifer A.G.M.

Cistus x laxus 'Snow White'

Cistus x pulverulentus 'Sunset'

Cistus 'Elma' A.G.M (Cistaceae)

Common name: None
Height: 6ft (1.8m)
Spread: 6ft (1.8m)
Aspect: Full sun
Soil: Well-drained
Hardiness: Zone 8
Propagation: Softwood or greenwood
cuttings in summer
Flowering time: All summer

A bushy shrub. Leaves lance-shaped, glossy-
green. Flowers in terminal cymes of up to 6,
white, yellow stamens. Prune after flowering
only by deadheading, and to keep symmetry.

- Drought-tolerant
- Evergreen
- Requires space
- Short-lived

Cistus ladanifer A.G.M. (Cistaceae)

Common name: Gum rock rose
Height: 6ft (1.8m)
Spread: 5ft (1.5m)
Aspect: Full sun
Soil: Well-drained
Hardiness: Zone 8
Propagation: Seed as soon as ripe; softwood
or greenwood cuttings in summer
Flowering time: All summer

An upright shrub. Leaves aromatic, sticky,
lance-shaped, dark green. Flowers white,
with crimson marks at base of petals, borne
on side shoots. Prune for symmetry in
spring, and deadhead after flowering.

- Aromatic foliage
- Drought-tolerant
- Evergreen
- Requires space
- Short-lived

Cistus x laxus 'Snow White' (Cistaceae)

Common name: None
Height: 3ft (90cm)
Spread: 2ft (60cm)
Aspect: Full sun
Soil: Well-drained
Hardiness: Zone 8
Propagation: Softwood or greenwood
cuttings in summer
Flowering time: Early spring and summer.

A hybrid, evergreen shrub. Leaves
ovate/lanceolate, viscid, pubescent, green.
Flowers white, with yellow centers. Prune
for symmetry in spring; deadhead after
flowering.

- Drought-tolerant
- Evergreen
- Short-lived

Cistus x pulverulentus 'Sunset' (Cistaceae)

Common name: None
Height: 3ft (90cm)
Spread: 2ft (60cm)
Aspect: Full sun
Soil: Well-drained
Hardiness: Zone 8
Propagation: Softwood or greenwood
cuttings in summer
Flowering time: All summer

An evergreen, compact shrub. Leaves
oblong, gray-green. Flowers in terminal
cymes, rose-pink, with yellow centers, borne
profusely. Very desirable. Deadhead after
flowering, and prune for shape, in spring.

- Drought-tolerant
- Evergreen
- Handsome foliage
- Short-lived

Cistus x *skanbergii* A.G.M.

Cuphea cyanea

Colutea arborescens

Coronilla valentina ssp. *glauca* A.G.M.

Cistus x *skanbergii* A.G.M. (Cistaceae)

Common name: None
Height: 30in (75cm)
Spread: 3ft (90cm)
Aspect: Full sun
Soil: Well-drained
Hardiness: Zone 8
Propagation: Softwood or greenwood cuttings in summer
Flowering time: All summer

An evergreen, hybrid shrub. Leaves lance-shaped, gray-green. Flowers pale pink, in terminal cymes of up to 6, borne profusely. Deadhead after flowering.

- Drought-tolerant
- Short-lived
- Evergreen

Colutea arborescens (Leguminosae)

Common name: Bladder-senna
Height: 10ft (3m)
Spread: 10ft (3m)
Aspect: Full sun
Soil: Well-drained, fertile
Hardiness: Zone 5
Propagation: Seed in spring; greenwood cuttings in summer
Flowering time: Long period in summer

A robust shrub. Leaves pale green, pinnate. Flowers in racemes of up to 8, pea-like, yellow, followed by inflated, transparent seed pods. *Colutea* x *media* (Zone 6) is similar.

- Requires space
- Seeds everywhere

Coronilla valentina ssp. *glauca* A.G.M. (Papilionaceae)

Common name: None
Height: 32in (80cm)
Spread: 32in (80cm)
Aspect: Full sun
Soil: Well-drained, fertile
Hardiness: Zone 9
Propagation: Seed in heat in spring
Flowering time: Late winter and early spring; late summer

A rounded, very compact shrub. Leaves pinnate, blue-green. Flowers in axillary umbels of up to 14, fragrant, pea-like, bright yellow. Prune minimally by removing only wayward shoots; cut to near ground if too leggy.

- Evergreen
- Handsome foliage
- Scented flowers

Cuphea cyanea (Lythraceae)

Common name: None
Height: 4ft (1.2m)
Spread: 3ft (90cm)
Aspect: Full sun, but not midday
Soil: Well-drained, fertile
Hardiness: Zone 9
Propagation: Seed in warmth, or division, both in spring
Flowering time: Late spring to autumn

A branching subshrub, with ovate mid-green leaves. Flowers are borne in terminal racemes, tubular, orange-red, with green tips. Prune in spring to within 1in (2.5cm) of previous year's growth.

- Attracts bees

Cuphea ignea A.G.M.

Cuphea ignea A.G.M. (Lythraceae)

Common name: Cigarflower
Height: 30in (75cm)
Spread: 3ft (90cm)
Aspect: Full sun, but not midday
Soil: Well-drained, fertile
Hardiness: Zone 9
Propagation: Seed in heat, or division, in spring
Flowering time: Late spring to autumn

A spreading shrub. Leaves glossy-green. Flowers solitary, long slim tubules, deep red with a dark red band and a white rim. Prune in spring by cutting back to within 1in (2.5cm) of previous year's growth.

• Attracts bees

CYTISUS (Leguminosae)
Broom

A genus of some 50 species of evergreen/deciduous shrubs; in nature they grow invariably on well-drained, acid sites. Brooms flower abundantly, the flowers being pea-like, sometimes fragrant, and borne in terminal, leafy, axillary racemes, or singly. Many hybrids are in cultivation. They are low-allergen plants, suitable for gardeners with allergies. Brooms are drought-tolerant and thrive on poor soils. They should be pruned to remove wayward growths, and cut back annually after flowering to strong buds low down, or to young side shoots; they must not be pruned hard when mature. Brooms flower over the period from mid/late spring to early summer. All parts are poisonous, especially the seeds.

Cytisus 'Goldfinch'

Cytisus 'La Coquette'

Cytisus 'Goldfinch' (Leguminosae)

Common name: Broom
Height: 5ft (1.5m)
Spread: 5ft (1.5m)
Aspect: Full sun
Soil: Acid, well-drained
Hardiness: Zone 6
Propagation: Ripewood cuttings in midsummer
Flowering time: Late spring to early summer

A compact, medium-sized, deciduous, hybrid shrub. Flowers are pale cream, with dark cerise wings, and the reverse of the petal is cerise.

• Drought-tolerant • Poisonous
• Low allergen

Cytisus 'La Coquette' (Leguminosae)

Common name: None
Height: 5ft (1.5m)
Spread: 5ft (1.5m)
Aspect: Full sun
Soil: Acid, well-drained.
Hardiness: Zone 6
Propagation: Ripewood cuttings in midsummer
Flowering time: Late spring to early summer

A compact, medium-sized, deciduous, hybrid shrub. Flowers are rose-red, yellow inside; the wings are deep orange, and the keel pale yellow, with rose-red markings.

• Drought-tolerant • Poisonous
• Low allergen

Cytisus 'Lena' A.G.M. (Leguminosae)

Common name: None
Height: 4ft (1.2m)
Spread: 5ft (1.5m)
Aspect: Full sun
Soil: Acid, well-drained
Hardiness: Zone 6
Propagation: Ripewood cuttings in midsummer
Flowering time: Late spring to early summer

A spreading, but compact, deciduous, hybrid shrub. Flowers deep yellow, with the wings and the reverse of the standards bright red, in axillary clusters.

• Drought-tolerant • Poisonous
• Low allergen

Cytisus 'Lena' A.G.M.

Cytisus nigricans (Leguminosae)

Common name: None
Height: 5ft (1.5m)
Spread: 3ft (90cm)
Aspect: Full sun
Soil: Acid, well-drained
Hardiness: Zone 5
Propagation: Ripewood cuttings in midsummer
Flowering time: Late summer

An upright, deciduous species. Leaves tri-palmate. Flowers yellow, in terminal racemes.

- Drought-tolerant
- Low allergen
- Poisonous

Cytisus praecox albus (Leguminosae)

Common name: Warminster broom
Height: 5ft (1.5m)
Spread: 4ft (1.2m)
Aspect: Full sun
Soil: Acid, well-drained
Hardiness Zone 5
Propagation: Ripewood cuttings in summer
Flowering time: Mid and late spring

Compact, deciduous shrub. Flowers in axillary clusters, white, pendent, on arching stems.

- Drought-tolerant
- Low allergen
- Poisonous

Daboecia cantabrica ssp. scotica 'Silverwells' A.G.M. (Ericaceae)

Common name: Irish heath
Height: 6in (15cm)
Spread: 20in (50cm)
Aspect: Sun or part shade
Soil: Acid, well-drained
Hardiness: Zone 6
Propagation: Ripewood cuttings in summer
Flowering time: Early summer to mid-autumn

A dwarf, compact, ericaceous shrub. Leaves shiny dark green above, densely hairy-silver below. Flowers in racemes, white, pendent. Prune in spring by cutting back flowered shoots to within 1in (2.5cm) of previous year's growth.

- Evergreen

Daboecia cantabrica ssp. scotica 'William Buchanan' A.G.M. (Ericaceae)

Common name: None
Height: 15in (38cm)
Spread: 2ft (60cm)
Aspect: Sun or part shade
Soil: Acid, well-drained
Hardiness: Zone 6
Propagation: Semi-ripe cuttings in midsummer
Flowering time: Early summer to late autumn

A compact, ericaceous shrub. Flowers in racemes, ovoid urns, crimson-purple. Prune in spring by cutting back to within 1in (2.5cm) of previous year's growth.

- Evergreen

Daboecia cantabrica 'Silverwells' A.G.M.

Cytisus praecox albus

Cytisus nigricans

Daboecia cantabrica ssp. *scotica* 'William Buchanan' A.G.M.

Dendromecon rigida (Papaveraceae)

Common name: Bush-poppy
Height: 10ft (3m)
Spread: 10ft (3m)
Aspect: Full sun
Soil: Well-drained
Hardiness: Zone 8
Propagation: Seed in heat, in spring;
softwood cuttings in summer
Flowering time: Spring to autumn

A large, spreading, evergreen shrub. Leaves
leathery, gray-green. Flowers poppy-like,
solitary, scented, yellow. Cut back flowered
shoots after flowering to within 2, 3 or 4
buds of permanent framework.

- Evergreen
- Handsome foliage
- Scented flowers
- Requires space

Dendromecon rigida

Erica carnea 'Winter Snow'

ERICA (Ericaceae)
Heath

A genus of more than 700 species of
evergreen shrubs from a wide variety of
habitats in both hemispheres; most have
in common a need for soil which is acid
but some like it moist whilst others like
it dry. They may be prostrate or tree-
like. Of the 700 species, only a few (*EE
arborea*, *carnea*, *cinerea*, x *darleyensis*,
erigena and *vagans*) are widespread in
cultivation, and many clones of these
are to be found in the catalogues: some
73 cultivars have earned the Award of
Garden merit of the Royal Horticultural
Society.

The flower of the heath can be
distinguished from that of the heather
by its prominent corolla and calyces
(usually of green). All require full sun,
with the notable exception of *E. vagans*.
Erica cultivars require to be cut back
after flowering to within 1in (2.5cm) of
the previous year's growth. The lengthy
listing of A.G.M. varieties is omitted,
and the interested reader is referred to
the specialist nurserymen's catalogues.

Erica cinerea 'C.D. Eason' A.G.M.

Erica cinerea 'Domino'

Erica carnea 'Winter Snow' (Ericaceae)

Common name: Spring heath
Height: 6in (15cm)
Spread: 18in (45cm)
Aspect: Sun or part shade
Soil: Acid, well-drained
Hardiness: Zone 5
Propagation: Semi-ripe cuttings in mid to
late summer
Flowering time: Late winter and early spring

A low, spreading shrub with dark green
leaves. Flowers white, urn-shaped, in one-
sided racemes. Will tolerate alkaline soil,
only if mildly so.

- Evergreen
- Low allergen

Erica cinerea 'C.D. Eason' A.G.M.
(Ericaceae)

Common name: None
Height: 10in (25cm)
Spread: 20in (50cm)
Aspect: Sun
Soil: Acid, well-drained
Hardiness: Zone 5
Propagation: Semi-ripe cuttings in mid- to
late summer
Flowering time: Early summer to autumn

A clone which is good ground cover. Leaves
dark green. Flowers urn-shaped, bright
magenta, in racemes.

- Evergreen
- Low allergen

Erica cinerea 'Domino' (Ericaceae)

Common name: None
Height: 2ft (60cm)
Spread: 32in (80cm)
Aspect: Sun
Soil: Acid, well-drained
Hardiness: Zone 5
Propagation: Semi-ripe cuttings in mid- to
late summer
Flowering time: Early summer to autumn

A clone with dark, bottle-green leaves.
Flowers urn-shaped, white, in racemes.

- Evergreen
- Low allergen

Erica cinerea 'Pink Ice' A.G.M.

Erica x darleyensis 'George Rendall'

Erica cinerea 'Stephen Davis' A.G.M. (Ericaceae)

Common name: None
Height: 8in (20cm)
Spread: 15in (38cm)
Aspect: Sun
Soil: Acid, well-drained
Hardiness: Zone 5
Propagation: Semi-ripe cuttings in mid- to late summer
Flowering time: Early summer to autumn

A striking clone. Foliage dark green. Flower vivid dark pink, in racemes.

● Evergreen
● Low allergen

Erica x darleyensis 'Darley Dale' (Ericaceae)

Common name: Darley heath
Height: 1ft (30cm)
Spread: 20in (50cm)
Aspect: Sun
Soil: Acid, well-drained
Hardiness: Zone 6
Propagation: Semi-ripe cuttings in mid- to late summer
Flowering time: Late winter and early spring

A bushy, ericaceous shrub. Leaves mid-green, tipped cream in spring. Flowers urn-shaped, shell pink, darkening with time, in racemes. Good ground cover.

● Evergreen
● Handsome foliage
● Low allergen

Erica cinerea 'Stephen Davis' A.G.M.

Erica x darleyensis 'Darley Dale'

Erica cinerea 'Pink Ice' A.G.M. (Ericaceae)

Common name: None
Height: 8in (20cm)
Spread: 14in (35cm)
Aspect: Sun
Soil: Acid, well-drained
Hardiness: Zone 5
Propagation: Semi-ripe cuttings in mid- to late summer
Flowering time: Early summer to autumn

A twiggy, dwarf clone. Leaves bronze in winter, deep green in summer. Flowers clear pink, urn-shaped, in racemes.

● Evergreen
● Low allergen

Erica x darleyensis 'George Rendall' (Ericaceae)

Common name: Darley heath
Height: 1ft (30cm)
Spread: 2ft (60cm)
Aspect: Sun
Soil: Acid, well-drained
Hardiness: Zone 6
Propagation: Semi-ripe cuttings in mid- to late summer
Flowering time: Late winter to early spring

A very handsome clone. Leaves mid-green, lance-shaped. Flowers urn-shaped, rich pink, in racemes.

● Evergreen
● Low allergen

Erica erigena 'Irish Dusk' A.G.M. (Ericaceae)

Common name: None
Height: 2ft (60cm)
Spread: 18in (45cm)
Aspect: Sun
Soil: Acid, well-drained
Hardiness: Zone 8
Propagation: Semi-ripe cuttings in mid- to late summer
Flowering time: Late autumn to late spring

A half-hardy, ericaceous shrub. Leaves dark gray-green. Flowers urn-shaped, honey-scented, rose-pink.

- Evergreen
- Handsome foliage
- Low allergen
- Scented flowers

Erica erigena 'Irish Dusk' A.G.M.   *Erica gracilis*

Erica gracilis (Ericaceae)

Common name: None
Height: 20in (50cm)
Spread: 20in (50cm)
Aspect: Sun
Soil: Acid, well-drained
Hardiness: Zone 10
Propagation: Semi-ripe cuttings in mid- to late summer
Flowering time: Autumn to spring

A very tender, compact shrub from S. Africa. Flowers urn-shaped, cerise, pink or white, in whorls of 4. Requires warm greenhouse or conservatory in cold areas.

- Evergreen
- Low allergen

Erysimum 'Bowles' Mauve' (Brassicaceae)

Common name: Wallflower
Height: 42in (1m)
Spread: 2ft (60cm)
Aspect: Sun
Soil: Well-drained, fertile
Hardiness: Zone 7
Propagation: Softwood cuttings, with a heel, in spring or summer
Flowering time: Early spring to autumn

Erysimum 'Bowles' Mauve'

An evergreen, woody subshrub, with gray-green leaves. Flowers mauve, in racemes. Short-lived, and less floriferous with age.

- Drought-tolerant
- Evergreen
- Handsome foliage
- Attracts slugs
- Must deadhead
- Prone to mildew
- Short-lived

Euryops pectinatus A.G.M. (Asteraceae)

Common name: None
Height: 3ft (90cm)
Spread: 3ft (90cm)
Aspect: Full sun
Soil: Well-drained, fertile
Hardiness: Zone 8
Propagation: Seed in heat in spring; semi-ripe cuttings in summer
Flowering time: Early summer to autumn; into winter in mild areas

A half-hardy shrub. Leaves pinnatisect, hairy, gray. Flowers single or in clusters, on long stems, yellow. Prune lightly after flowering.

- Good cut flower
- Highly allergenic

Euryops pectinatus A.G.M.

Fremontodendron californicum
(Sterculiaceae)

Common name: Flannel-bush
Height: 20ft (6m)
Spread: 12ft (4m)
Aspect: Full sun
Soil: Well-drained, fertile
Hardiness: Zone 8
Propagation: Seed in heat in spring
Flowering time: Late spring to mid-autumn

A half-hardy, semi-evergreen or evergreen shrub. Leaves dark green. Flowers large, single, yellow saucers.

- Drought-tolerant
- Highly allergenic
- Requires space
- Skin irritant

Fremontodendron californicum

Fuchsia 'Bicentennial'

FUCHSIA (Onagraceae)
Fuchsia

A genus of only some 100 or so species, but over 8,000 hybrids are in cultivation. The genus is renowned for its free-flowering and long-flowering qualities: it flowers from summer to late autumn. Degree of hardiness varies within the genus, from Zone 6 to Zone 9, so it is important to check the hardiness before buying a plant. The pendent flower is quite unique: the upper part is composed of sepals which form a perianth tube, at the lower end of which the sepals are spread out. Below is a cup- or bell-shaped corolla formed by the petals; in some species the petals are absent, or much reduced. The number of petals varies from 4, in single flowers, through 5–7 in double flowers, to 8 or more in fully double flowers. The perianth and corolla can be the same color or different colors. The flowers are followed by berries, usually containing many seeds. Fuchsias may be evergreen or deciduous, and the leaves are lance-shaped to ovate, usually toothed and mid-green, although a number of handsome variegated cultivars are in cultivation. They should be cut back to their permanent framework in early spring. An Award of Garden merit of the Royal Horticultural Society has been given to 56 Fuchsias.

Fuchsia 'Bicentennial' (Onagaaceae)

Common name: None
Height: 18in (45cm)
Spread: 2ft (60cm)
Aspect: Sun or part shade
Soil: Moist, well-drained
Hardiness: Zone 9
Propagation: Softwood cuttings in spring
Flowering time: Summer to late autumn

A tender Fuchsia, with arching stems bearing fully double flowers, with pale orange-pink sepals and magenta petals.

- Attracts bees
- Low allergen

Fuchsia 'Coralle' A.G.M. (Onagraceae)

Common name: None
Height: 3ft (90cm)
Spread: 2ft (60cm)
Aspect: Sun or part shade
Soil: Moist, well-drained
Hardiness: Zone 9
Propagation: Softwood cuttings in spring
Flowering time: Midsummer to late autumn

A tender Fuchsia. Leaves olive-green, velvety. Flowers in terminal clusters, with upturned sepals and tubes of orange-red, and corollas of salmon-pink.

- Attracts bees
- Low allergen

Fuchsia 'Coralle' A.G.M.

Fuchsia 'Happy Wedding'

Fuchsia 'Love's Reward'

Fuchsia 'Lye's Unique'

Fuchsia 'Madame Cornelissen'

Fuchsia 'Happy Wedding' (Onagraceae)

Common name: None
Height: 1ft (30cm)
Spread: 18in (45cm)
Aspect: Sun or half shade
Soil: Moist, well-drained, fertile
Hardiness: Zone 8
Propagation: Softwood cuttings, in spring
Flowering time: Summer to late autumn

A half-hardy cultivar. Flowers semi-double, tube and sepals in shell pink.

- Attracts bees
- Low allergen

Fuchsia 'Love's Reward' (Onagraceae)

Common name: None
Height: 18in (45cm)
Spread: 18in (45cm)
Aspect: Sun or part shade
Soil: Moist, well-drained, fertile
Hardiness: Zone 8
Propagation: Softwood cuttings in spring
Flowering time: Summer to late autumn

An upright shrub with single, medium-sized flowers. Sepals and tubes pale pink, corollas of violet-blue.

- Attracts bees
- Low allergen

Fuchsia 'Lye's Unique' (Onagraceae)

Common name: None
Height: 2ft (60cm)
Spread: 18in (45cm)
Aspect: Sun or half shade
Soil: Moist, well-drained, fertile
Hardiness: Zone 8
Propagation: Softwood cuttings in spring
Flowering time: Summer to autumn

A free-flowering shrub. Flowers single, sepals and tubes of white, corollas of deep salmon.

- Attracts bees
- Low allergen

Fuchsia 'Madame Cornelissen' (Onagraceae)

Common name: None
Height: 3ft (90cm)
Spread: 1ft (30cm)
Aspect: Sun or half shade
Soil: Moist, well-drained, fertile
Hardiness: Zone 6
Propagation: Softwood cuttings in spring
Flowering time: Summer to late autumn

A hardy shrub. Flowers double or semi-double, with red tubes and sepals, and a corolla of pure white.

- Attracts bees
- Low allergen

Fuchsia 'Thalia' A.G.M.

Grevillea 'Canberra Gem' A.G.M.

Fuchsia 'Phenomenal' (Onagraceae)

Common name: None
Height: 1ft (30cm)
Spread: 1ft (30cm)
Aspect: Sun or part shade
Soil: Moist, well-drained, fertile
Hardiness: Zone 7
Propagation: Softwood cuttings in spring
Flowering time: Summer to late autumn

A hardy Fuchsia with very large, double flowers. Sepals and tube red, corolla mauve-purple.

* Attracts bees
* Low allergen

Fuchsia 'Phenomenal'

Fuchsia 'Reading Show' (Onagraceae)

Common name: None
Height: 1ft (30cm)
Spread: 1ft (30cm)
Aspect: Sun or part shade
Soil: Moist, well-drained, fertile
Hardiness: Zone 8
Propagation: Softwood cuttings in spring
Flowering time: Midsummer to late autumn

A handsome, large-flowered cultivar. Flowers have tube and sepals of bright red, and a deep blue corolla.

* Attracts bees
* Low allergen

Fuchsia 'Thalia' A.G.M. (Onagraceae)

Common name: None
Height: 3ft (90cm)
Spread: 3ft (90cm)
Aspect: Sun or part shade
Soil: Moist, well-drained, fertile
Hardiness: Zone 9
Propagation: Softwood cuttings in spring
Flowering time: Midsummer to late autumn

A very desirable cultivar. Flowers very long-tubed, borne in profusion in terminal clusters. Flowers have red tubes and sepals, and orange petals. Tender.

* Attracts bees
* Low allergen

Grevillea 'Canberra Gem' A.G.M. (Proteaceae)

Common name: None
Height: 12ft (4m)
Spread: 15ft (4.5m)
Aspect: Full sun
Soil: Acid or neutral, fertile
Hardiness: Zone 9
Propagation: Semi-ripe cuttings in summer
Flowering time: Late winter to late summer, but also at other times

A large, tender shrub. Leaves linear, green above, hairy-silky below. Flowers petalless, calyx red, waxy, in dense racemes. Prune in early spring by removing wayward shoots.

* Evergreen
* Handsome foliage
* Requires space
* Skin irritant

Fuchsia 'Reading Show'

Grevillea rosmarinifolia A.G.M.

Grindelia chiloensis

Hebe albicans A.G.M.

Hebe x *franciscana* 'Blue Gem' A.G.M.

HEBE (Scrophulariaceae)
Hebe

A genus of about 100 evergreen shrubs, grown usually for their evergreen foliage value, but some are reasonably long-flowering. They vary in their degree of hardiness from tender to fully hardy. They like sun or part shade but dislike cold, drying winds. They are excellent seaside plants. Soil should be moist, but well-drained and not too rich. Most hebes require very little pruning.

Hebe albicans A.G.M. (Scrophulariaceae)

Common name: None
Height: 2ft (60cm)
Spread: 3ft (90cm)
Aspect: Sun or part shade
Soil: Moist, well-drained
Hardiness: Zone 8
Propagation: Seed when ripe; semi-ripe cuttings in late summer
Flowering time: Early and midsummer

A mound-forming, evergreen shrub. Leaves gray-green. Flowers white, medium-sized, in short terminal racemes. Prune by deadheading, and to preserve symmetry.

● Evergreen   ● Prone to mildew
● Handsome foliage
● Low allergen

Grevillea rosmarinifolia A.G.M.
(Proteaceae)

Common name: None
Height: 10ft (3m)
Spread: 15ft (4.5m)
Aspect: Full sun
Soil: Acid to neutral, fertile
Hardiness: Zone 9
Propagation: Semi-ripe cuttings in summer
Flowering time: Early spring to late summer

A large, tender, evergreen shrub. Leaves narrow, gray-green above, downy-silky below. Flowers petalless, calyx pink or yellow, in racemes. Prune to keep shape and size.

● Evergreen   ● Requires space
● Handsome foliage   ● Skin irritant

Grindelia chiloensis (Asteraceae)

Common name: None
Height: 3ft (90cm)
Spread: 3ft (90cm)
Aspect: Sun
Soil: Well-drained
Hardiness: Zone 6
Propagation: Seed in spring; semi-ripe cuttings in summer
Flowering time: All summer

An evergreen subshrub. Basal rosette of gray-green leaves. Flowers solitary, semi-double, yellow, on long stems. Minimal pruning.

● Drought-tolerant   ● Requires staking
● Evergreen
● Good cut flower

Hebe x *franciscana* 'Blue Gem' A.G.M.
(Scrophulariaceae)

Common name: None
Height: 5ft (1.5m)
Spread: 5ft (1.5m)
Aspect: Sun or part shade
Soil: Moist, well-drained
Hardiness: Zone 7
Propagation: Semi-ripe cuttings with bottom heat in late summer
Flowering time: Summer to autumn

A spreading shrub. Leaves mid-green. Flowers mauve, in dense axillary racemes. Prune by deadheading, and to preserve symmetry.

● Evergreen
● Low allergen

Hebe 'Great Orme' A.G.M.

Hebe 'Great Orme' A.G.M. (Scrophulariaceae)

Common name: None
Height: 4ft (1.2m)
Spread: 4ft (1.2m)
Aspect: Sun or part shade
Soil: Moist, well-drained
Hardiness: Zone 8
Propagation: Semiripe cuttings with bottom heat in late summer
Flowering time: Midsummer to mid-autumn

An evergreen, open shrub. Leaves glossy-green. Flowers bright pink, ageing to white, borne on dense axillary spikes.

- Evergreen
- Handsome foliage
- Low allergen

Hebe 'Youngii'

Hebe 'Youngii' (Scrophulariaceae)

Common name: None
Height: 8in (20cm)
Spread: 2ft (60cm)
Aspect: Sun or part shade
Soil: Moist, well-drained
Hardiness: Zone 8
Propagation: Semi-ripe cuttings, with bottom heat, in late summer
Flowering time: Several weeks in summer

An evergreen, mat-forming shrub. Leaves dark green, perhaps margined red. Flowers large, violet with white throats, in axillary racemes. Prune by deadheading, and to preserve symmetry.

- Evergreen
- Low allergen

Helianthemum 'Ben Hope' (Cistaceae)

Common name: Sunrose
Height: 1ft (30cm)
Spread: 1ft (30cm)
Aspect: Sun
Soil: Well-drained, fertile
Hardiness: Zone 6
Propagation: Softwood cuttings in late spring/early summer
Flowering time: Late spring to early summer

A spreading shrub. Leaves pale gray-green, downy. Flowers single, saucer-shaped, red, with orange centers, in raceme-like cymes. After flowering, cut back flowered shoots to within 1in (2.5cm) of previous year's growth.

- Drought-tolerant
- Evergreen
- Low allergen

Helianthemum 'Coppernob' (Cistaceae)

Common name: Sunrose
Height: 1ft (30cm)
Spread: 1ft (30cm)
Aspect: Sun
Soil: Well-drained, fertile
Hardiness: Zone 6
Propagation: Softwood cuttings in late spring/early summer
Flowering time: Mid-spring to summer

A charming, creeping subshrub. Leaves gray-green. Flowers of deep copper, with a bronze-crimson center, in cymes. After flowering, cut back flowered shoots to within 1in (2.5cm) of previous year's growth.

- Drought-tolerant
- Evergreen
- Low allergen

Helianthemum 'Coppernob'

Helianthemum 'Ben Hope'

Helianthemum 'Fireball' (Cistaceae)

Common name: Sunrose
Height: 8in (20cm)
Spread: 1ft (30cm)
Aspect: Full sun
Soil: Well-drained, fertile
Hardiness: Zone 6
Propagation: Softwood cuttings from spring to early summer
Flowering time: Late spring to midsummer

An evergreen subshrub. Leaves gray-green. Flowers fully double, bright red, in cymes. After flowering, cut back flowered shoots to within 1in (2.5cm) of previous year's growth.

- Drought-tolerant
- Evergreen
- Low allergen

Helianthemum 'Raspberry Ripple' (Cistaceae)

Common name: Sunrose
Height: 8in (20cm)
Spread: 1ft (30cm)
Aspect: Full sun
Soil: Well-drained, fertile
Hardiness: Zone 6
Propagation: Softwood cuttings from spring to early summer
Flowering time: Late spring to midsummer

A very attractive, evergreen subshrub. Leaves dark gray-green. Flowers white, with purple-pink centers, the color radiating to the margins of the petals. After flowering, cut back flowered shoots to within 1in (2.5cm) of previous year's growth.

- Drought-tolerant
- Evergreen
- Low allergen

Hibiscus rosa-sinensis hybridus (Malvaceae)

Common name: None
Height: 15ft (4.5m)
Spread: 10ft (3m)
Aspect: Full sun
Soil: Moist, well-drained, humus-rich
Hardiness: Zone 9
Propagation: Seed in heat, or softwood cuttings, in spring
Flowering time: Summer to autumn

A large, tender evergreen shrub, with glossy-green leaves. Flowers solitary, single, 5-petaled, in a range of colors or bicolored (as below, left). Minimal pruning required.

- Evergreen
- Handsome foliage
- Low allergen
- Prone to mildew
- Requires space

Helianthemum 'Fireball'

Hibiscus rosa-sinensis hybridus (Malvaceae)

Common name: None
Height: 15ft (4.5m)
Spread: 10ft (3m)
Aspect: Full sun
Soil: Moist, well-drained, humus-rich
Hardiness: Zone 9
Propagation: Seed in heat, or greenwood cuttings, in spring
Flowering time: Summer to autumn

Large, tender evergreen shrub, with glossy-green leaves. Flowers solitary, 5-petaled, single (yellow and reflexed, as below, right), in a range of colors. Minimal pruning required.

- Evergreen
- Handsome foliage
- Low allergen
- Prone to mildew
- Requires space

Helianthemum 'Raspberry Ripple'

Hibiscus rosa-sinensis hybridus (1)

Hibiscus rosa-sinensis hybridus (2)

Hibiscus syriacus 'Hamabo' A.G.M.

Hibiscus syriacus 'Blue Bird' A.G.M.
(Malvaceae)

Common name: Shrub althea
Height: 8ft (2.5m)
Spread: 4ft (1.2m)
Aspect: Full sun
Soil: Moist, well-drained, humus-rich
Hardiness: Zone 5
Propagation: Softwood cuttings in late spring
Flowering time: Late summer to mid-autumn

A medium-sized, hardy, deciduous shrub. Leaves toothed, dark green. Flowers large, single or in pairs, blue with red centers.

- Low allergen
- Prone to mildew
- Requires space

Hibiscus syriacus 'Hamabo' A.G.M.
(Malvaceae)

Common name: None
Height: 8ft (2.5m)
Spread: 4ft (1.2m)
Aspect: Sun
Soil: Moist, humus-rich, well-drained
Hardiness: Zone 5
Propagation: Softwood cuttings in late spring
Flowering time: Late summer to mid-autumn

A medium-sized, hardy, deciduous shrub. Flowers single, large, pale pink with a crimson eye. Minimal pruning required.

- Low allergen
- Prone to mildew
- Requires space

HYDRANGEA (Hydrangeaceae)
Hydrangea

A genus of about 80 species from Asia, and both N. and S. America. The flowers may be in corymbs or panicles, composed of large sterile flowers and small fertile flowers. The cultivars of the common Hydrangea, *Hydrangea macrophylla*, can be divided into two groups:

Hortensias: These 'mophead' cultivars have rounded flowerheads, composed of sterile flowers.

Lacecaps: These have flattened flowerheads, with fertile, small central flowers, surrounded by large sterile flowers.

Additionally, some cultivars of *Hydrangea serrata* are also called 'Lacecaps', and this is the best species for small gardens (see *H. serrata* 'Bluebird').
   The color of flower depends upon the availability of ions of aluminium in the ground. Blue flowers ensue when the soil is acid at a pH of below 5.5. Pink flowers ensue when the pH is greater than 5.5. White flowers are not influenced by pH. Flower color can be manipulated artificially by the use of a 'blueing' compound.
   Hydrangeas may be evergreen or deciduous; some are climbers and others are trees. All parts are poisonous, and contact with foliage may irritate the skin. The flower heads can be dried for winter decoration.

Hibiscus syriacus 'Blue Bird' A.G.M.

Hydrangea macrophylla 'Leuchtfeuer'

Hydrangea macrophylla 'Blaumeise'

Hydrangea macrophylla 'Blaumeise'
(Hydrangeaceae)

Common name: None
Height: 6ft (1.8m)
Spread: 8ft (2.5m)
Aspect: Sun or part shade
Soil: Moist, well-drained, fertile
Hardiness: Zone 5
Propagation: Softwood cuttings in early summer
Flowering time: Mid- and late summer

A Lacecap hydrangea. Leaves glossy, dark green. Flowers in flattened corymbs, with many central, cream-colored fertile flowers, and a few peripheral lilac-colored sterile flowers. Prune in early spring to the first bud below the flowerhead.

- Can be dried
- Low allergen
- Poisonous
- Prone to mildew
- Requires space
- Skin irritant

Hydrangea macrophylla 'Leuchtfeuer'
(Hydrangeaceae)

Common name: None
Height: 6ft (1.8m)
Spread: 6ft (1.8m)
Aspect: Sun or half shade
Soil: Moist, well-drained, fertile, humus-rich
Hardiness: Zone 5
Propagation: Softwood cuttings in early summer
Flowering time: Mid- and late summer

A Hortensia hydrangea. Leaves glossy green. Flowers in mopheads, large, sterile, cerise-pink. Prune in early spring by cutting back to the first bud below the flowerhead.

- Can be dried
- Low allergen
- Poisonous
- Prone to mildew
- Requires space
- Skin irritant

107

Hydrangea 'Sabrina' ®

Hydrangea 'Sandra' ®

Hydrangea 'Sabrina' ® (Hydrangeaceae)

Common name: None
Height: 4ft (1.2m)
Spread: 3ft (90cm)
Aspect: Sun or part shade
Soil: Moist, well-drained, humus-rich
Hardiness: Zone 5
Propagation: Softwood cuttings in early summer
Flowering time: Mid- and late summer

A Hortensia recently introduced from the Netherlands. Flowers in mopheads, large, sterile, pale pink with a darker edge. Prune in early spring by cutting back to the first bud below the flowerhead.

● Can be dried
● Low allergen
● Attracts slugs
● Poisonous
● Prone to mildew
● Skin irritant

Hydrangea 'Sandra' ® (Hydrangeaceae)

Common name: None
Height: 4ft (1.2m)
Spread: 3ft (90cm)
Aspect: Sun or part shade
Soil: Moist, well-drained, humus-rich
Hardiness: Zone 5
Propagation: Softwood cuttings in early summer
Flowering time: Mid- and late summer

A Lacecap recently introduced from the Netherlands. Flat corymbs of small central flowers, green, fading to white, and peripheral, large white flowers. Prune in early spring to the first bud below the flowerhead.

● Can be dried
● Low allergen
● Attracts slugs
● Poisonous
● Prone to mildew
● Skin irritant

Hydrangea paniculata (Hydrangeaceae)

Common name: Panicle hydrangea
Height: 22ft (7m)
Spread: 8ft (2.5m)
Aspect: Sun or part shade
Soil: Moist, well-drained, humus-rich
Hardiness: Zone 3
Propagation: Softwood cuttings in early summer
Flowering time: Late summer to autumn

A large, deciduous shrub. Conical panicles of small cream, fertile flowers, and large white, sterile flowers. In spring, prune previous year's shoots to within a few buds of the wood.

● Can be dried
● Low allergen
● Poisonous
● Prone to mildew
● Requires space

Hydrangea paniculata

Hydrangea serrata 'Bluebird' A.G.M. (Hydrangeaceae)

Common name: Tea-of-heaven
Height: 4ft (1.2m)
Spread: 4ft (1.2m)
Aspect: Sun or part shade
Soil: Moist, well-drained, humus-rich
Hardiness: Zone 6
Propagation: Softwood cuttings in early summer
Flowering time: Long period from summer to autumn

A compact cultivar. Leaves turn red in autumn. Lacecap corymbs of small, blue, fertile flowers surrounded by large, pale blue, sterile ones. Prune in early spring by cutting back to the first bud below the flowerhead.

● Can be dried
● Low allergen
● Attracts slugs
● Poisonous
● Prone to mildew
● Skin irritant

Hydrangea serrata 'Bluebird' A.G.M.

Hypericum calycinum

Hypericum x *inodorum* 'Elstead'

Iberis sempervirens

HYPERICUM (Clusiaceae)
Hypericum

A genus of over 400 species from all parts of the world; they may be annual, perennial or shrubs, evergreen or deciduous. The flowers are invariably yellow, with prominent yellow stamens, and are borne over long periods in some instances; some species have fruits after flowering. There is such a wide divergence in cultural requirement that it is difficult to generalize. Similarly, the shrubby species have quite different pruning requirements, depending on whether they are evergreen or deciduous. The dwarf species require full sun and sharp drainage, whereas the larger species will grow in sun or part shade, and also like well-drained soil.

Hypericum calycinum (Clusiaceae)

Common name: Rose of Sharon
Height: 2ft (60cm)
Spread: Indefinite
Aspect: Sun or part shade
Soil: Moist, well-drained
Hardiness: Zone 6
Propagation: Division in spring or autumn
Flowering time: Midsummer to mid-autumn

A rampant, evergreen shrub which spreads by runners. Flowers in cymes or single, yellow, saucer-shaped. Good ground cover, even in dry shade. Cut to the ground in spring.

- Drought-tolerant
- Evergreen
- Low allergen
- Invasive

Hypericum x inodorum 'Elstead' (Clusiaceae)

Common name: None
Height: 4ft (1.2m)
Spread: 4ft (1.2m)
Aspect: Sun or part shade
Soil: Moist, well-drained
Hardiness: Zone 8
Propagation: Greenwood or semi-ripe cuttings, in summer
Flowering time: Midsummer to mid-autumn

A bushy, semi-evergreen shrub with aromatic leaves. Flowers in cymes, small, star-shaped, yellow, followed by large red fruits. Prune in early spring by cutting back fairly hard to low wood.

- Handsome foliage
- Low allergen

Iberis sempervirens (Brassicaceae)

Common name: Evergreen candytuft
Height: 1ft (30cm)
Spread: 20in (50cm)
Aspect: Sun
Soil: Moist, well-drained, fertile
Hardiness: Zone 4
Propagation: Softwood cuttings in late spring
Flowering time: Late spring to early summer

An evergreen subshrub. Flowers small, in flat, corymb-like racemes, white, flushed pink perhaps. Cut back annually after flowering to within 1in (2.5cm) of previous year's growth.

- Attracts butterflies
- Evergreen
- Low allergen

Ixora coccinea (Rubiaceae)

Common name: None
Height: 6ft (1.8m)
Spread: 6ft (1.8m)
Aspect: Sun, but not at midday
Soil: Moist, fertile, well-drained; dry in winter
Hardiness: Zone 10
Propagation: Semi-ripe cuttings, with bottom heat, in summer
Flowering time: Late spring to early summer

A large, evergreen shrub. Flowers scented, 4-petaled, in corymb-like cymes, yellow, red, orange, or pink. Prune annually in spring by lightly cutting back.

- Evergreen
- Scented flowers
- Requires space

Ixora coccinea

Justicia carnea (Acanthaceae)

Common name: None
Height: 6ft (1.8m)
Spread: 3ft (90cm)
Aspect: Part shade
Soil: Moist, well-drained, fertile
Hardiness: Zone 10
Propagation: Seed in heat, or softwood cuttings, in spring
Flowering time: Summer and autumn

A tender, evergreen shrub. Leaves glossy-green. Flowers in dense, axillary or terminal spikes, 2-lipped, tubular, pink. Prune annually by deadheading, and light cutting back in spring.

- Evergreen
- Handsome foliage
- Requires space

Kerria japonica 'Pleniflora' A.G.M. (Rosaceae)

Common name: Kerria
Height: 10ft (3m)
Spread: 10ft (3m)
Aspect: Sun or part shade
Soil: Well-drained, fertile
Hardiness: Zone 4
Propagation: Greenwood cuttings in summer
Flowering time: Mid and late spring

A large, deciduous, spreading shrub. Flowers large, double, solitary, yellow. Prune annually after flowering by cutting back to strong buds, low down.

- Good cut flower
- Requires space

Lantana camara 'Radiation' (Verbenaceae)

Common name: Common lantana
Height: 6ft (1.8m)
Spread: 6ft (1.8m)
Aspect: Full sun
Soil: Moist, well-drained, fertile
Hardiness: Zone 10
Propagation: Semi-ripe cuttings with bottom heat, in summer
Flowering time: Late spring to late autumn

A tender, evergreen, medium-sized shrub. Flowers in flat heads, bicolored red and orange. Deadhead regularly, and remove wayward shoots in spring.

- Poisonous
- Prone to mildew
- Skin irritant

Lavandula stoechas A.G.M. (Lamiaceae)

Common name: French lavender
Height: 2ft (60cm)
Spread: 2ft (60cm)
Aspect: Sun
Soil: Well-drained, fertile
Hardiness: Zone 8
Propagation: Seed in spring; semi-ripe cuttings in summer
Flowering time: Late spring to early summer

A half-hardy, evergreen subshrub. Leaves gray-green, aromatic. Scented flowers, purple, in dense spikes topped by purple bracts. Cut flowered shoots back in spring to within 1in (2.5cm) of previous year's growth.

- Attracts bees
- Can be dried
- Evergreen
- Handsome foliage
- Scented flowers

Justicia carnea

Kerria japonica 'Pleniflora' A.G.M.

Lantana camara 'Radiation'

Lavandula stoechas A.G.M.

Lavatera 'Barnsley' A.G.M. (Malvaceae)

Common name: Herb tree-mallow
Height: 6ft (1.8m)
Spread: 4ft (1.2m)
Aspect: Sun
Soil: Well-drained, fertile
Hardiness: Zone 7
Propagation: Softwood cuttings in early summer
Flowering time: All summer

A short-lived, evergreen subshrub. Leaves gray-green. Flowers large, saucer-shaped, white with a red eye, in racemes. Prune in early spring by cutting back close to the base.

- Drought-tolerant
- Evergreen
- Good cut flower
- Handsome foliage
- Requires space
- Short-lived

Lavatera 'Bredon Springs' (Malvaceae)

Common name: Herb tree-mallow
Height: 6ft (1.8m)
Spread: 4ft (1.2m)
Aspect: Sun
Soil: Well-drained, fertile
Hardiness: Zone 8
Propagation: Softwood cuttings in early summer
Flowering time: All summer

A short-lived, evergreen subshrub. Leaves gray-green. Flowers large saucers, dusky pink, in racemes. Prune in early spring by cutting back hard, close to the base.

- Drought-tolerant
- Evergreen
- Good cut flower
- Handsome foliage
- Requires space
- Short-lived

Lavatera 'Burgundy Wine' (Malvaceae)

Common name: Herb tree-mallow
Height: 4ft (1.2m)
Spread: 3ft (90cm)
Aspect: Sun
Soil: Well-drained, fertile
Hardiness: Zone 7
Propagation: Softwood cuttings in early summer
Flowering time: All summer

A evergreen subshrub. Leaves gray-green. Flowers large, dark pink, with darker veins, in racemes. Suitable for a small garden. Prune in early spring by cutting back close to the base.

- Drought-tolerant
- Evergreen
- Good cut flower
- Handsome foliage
- Short-lived

Lavatera 'Candy Floss' (Malvaceae)

Common name: Herb tree-mallow
Height: 6ft (1.8m)
Spread: 4ft (1.2m)
Aspect: Sun
Soil: Well-drained, fertile
Hardiness: Zone 8
Propagation: Softwood cuttings in early summer
Flowering time: All summer

A short-lived, evergreen subshrub. Foliage gray-green. Flowers large, pale pink, saucer-shaped, in racemes. Prune in early spring by cutting back hard, close to the base.

- Drought-tolerant
- Evergreen
- Good cut flower
- Handsome foliage
- Requires space
- Short-lived

Lavatera 'Barnsley' A.G.M.

Lavatera 'Burgundy Wine'

Lavatera 'Candy Floss'

Lavatera 'Bredon Springs'

111

Leptospermum scoparium 'Nicholsii
Nanum' A.G.M. (Myrtaceae)

Common name: None
Height: 6in (15cm)
Spread: 18in (45cm)
Aspect: Sun or part shade
Soil: Well-drained, fertile
Hardiness: Zone 8
Propagation: Semi-ripe cuttings with bottom
heat, in summer
Flowering time: Late spring to early summer

A charming, dwarf, evergreen, half-hardy,
prostrate shrub. Leaves aromatic, green.
Flowers single, red, borne in profusion.
Prune after flowering only to deadhead and
maintain shape.

● Evergreen

Leptospermum scoparium 'Nicholsii Nanum' A.G.M.

Leptospermum scoparium 'Red Damask'
A.G.M. (Myrtaceae)

Common name: None
Height: 10ft (3m)
Spread: 10ft (3m)
Aspect: Sun or part shade
Soil: Well-drained, fertile
Hardiness: Zone 8
Propagation: Semi-ripe cuttings with bottom
heat in summer
Flowering time: Late spring to early summer

A large, half-hardy, evergreen shrub. Leaves
aromatic, dark green. Flowers solitary,
double, dark red, borne profusely. Prune
after flowering by deadheading, and to
preserve symmetry.

● Evergreen   ● Requires space

Leycesteria formosa (Caprifoliaceae)

Common name: Formosa-honeysuckle
Height: 6ft (1.8m)
Spread: 6ft (1.8m)
Aspect: Sun or part shade
Soil: Any well-drained, fertile
Hardiness: Zone 7
Propagation: Softwood cuttings in summer;
seed in autumn
Flowering time: Summer to early autumn

A tall, upright shrub with hollow, cane-like
stems. Flowers in pendent spikes, white,
surrounded by reddish-purple bracts,
followed by red berries. Prune annually in
spring, to medium or low framework.

● Requires space

Leptospermum scoparium 'Red Damask'   *Leycesteria formosa*

Lithodora diffusa 'Heavenly Blue'
(Boraginaceae)

Common name: None
Height: 6in (15cm)
Spread: 32in (80cm)
Aspect: Sun
Soil: Acidic, humus-rich
Hardiness: Zone 7
Propagation: Semi-ripe cuttings, in summer
Flowering time: Late spring to summer

An evergreen, prostrate subshrub. Flowers
deep blue, in terminal cymes. Prune after
flowering by cutting back flowered shoots
to within 1in (2.5cm) of previous year's
growth.

● Evergreen

Lithodora diffusa 'Heavenly Blue'

Lonicera x *brownii* 'Dropmore Scarlet'

Mimulus aurantiacus A.G.M.

Mimulus puniceus

Lupinus arboreus A.G.M.

Lonicera x *brownii* 'Dropmore Scarlet' (Caprifoliaceae)

Common name: None
Height: 12ft (4m)
Spread 30in (75cm)
Aspect: Sun or part shade
Soil: Moist, well-drained, humus-rich, fertile
Hardiness: Zone 5
Propagation: Greenwood cuttings in summer, hardwood cuttings in autumn
Flowering time: Long period in summer

A semi-evergreen, twining, climbing shrub. Leaves blue-green. Flowers bright scarlet, tubular, in terminal whorls. Regular pruning not necessary; prune only to fit to available space.

- Scented flowers
- Poisonous

Lupinus arboreus A.G.M. (Papilionaceae)

Common name: Tree lupine
Height: 6ft (1.8m)
Spread: 6ft (1.8m)
Aspect: Sun or part shade
Soil: Acid, sharply-drained
Hardiness: Zone 8
Propagation: Seed (after nicking and soaking) in spring or autumn
Flowering time: Late spring to midsummer

A bushy, evergreen subshrub. Leaves palmate, deeply-divided, gray-green. Flowers pea-like, scented, yellow, in upright racemes. Seeds poisonous.

- Evergreen
- Handsome foliage
- Scented flowers
- Poisonous
- Seeds everywhere

Mimulus aurantiacus A.G.M. (Scrophulariaceae)

Common name: Monkey-flower
Height: 3ft (90cm)
Spread: 3ft (90cm)
Aspect: Full sun
Soil: Well-drained, humus-rich
Hardiness: Zone 8
Propagation: Seed in autumn or spring; division, in autumn
Flowering time: Late summer to autumn

A small, evergreen shrub. Leaves sticky, glossy-green. Flowers trumpet-shaped, with wavy petal margins, red, yellow or orange, in leafy racemes. Prune in spring by deadheading and by removing wayward shoots.

- Evergreen
- Handsome foliage
- Low allergen
- Prone to mildew
- Short-lived

Mimulus puniceus (Scrophulariaceae)

Common name: None
Height: 5ft (1.5m)
Spread: 5ft (1.5m)
Aspect: Full sun
Soil: Well-drained, humus-rich, fertile
Hardiness: Zone 9
Propagation: Softwood cuttings in early summer, or semi-ripe cuttings in midsummer
Flowering time: Spring to late summer

A tender shrub from Mexico and California. Flowers orange red, in leafy racemes. Prune in spring by deadheading and by removing wayward shoots.

- Low allergen
- Attracts slugs
- Prone to mildew

Nerium oleander

Osteospermum 'Buttermilk' A.G.M.

Nicotiana glauca (Solanaceae)

Common name: Tree tobacco
Height: 10ft (3m)
Spread: 10ft (3m)
Aspect: Sun or part shade
Soil: Moist, well-drained, fertile
Hardiness: Zone 8
Propagation: Seed in heat in spring
Flowering time: Long periods in summer

A fast-growing, large, half-hardy, evergreen shrub. Leaves blue-gray. Flowers narrow tubular, bright yellow. Cut back in early spring to low permanent framework.

- Evergreen
- Handsome foliage
- Requires space
- Skin irritant

OSTEOSPERMUM (Asteraceae)
Osteospermum

A genus of about 70 evergreen species from Arabia and South Africa; they are mostly tender or half-hardy, but a few are hardy. The flowers are daisy-like, single, and solitary or borne in panicles. Flowering is from late spring to autumn, especially if deadheaded. The color range is wide, and some have differing ray and disc florets. They must be given a sunny position as the flowers do not open in the shade. A large number of hybrids are coming into cultivation.
Osteospermums make excellent ground cover where they can be left in the open all year round. They make good cut flowers, but are highly allergenic and prone to downy mildew.

Nicotiana glauca

Nerium oleander (Apocynaceae)

Common name: Oleander
Height: 20ft (6m)
Spread: 9ft (2.7m)
Aspect: Sun
Soil: Moist, well-drained, fertile, dry in winter
Hardiness: Zone 9
Propagation: Semi-ripe cuttings, with bottom heat, in summer
Flowering time: Several weeks in summer

An evergreen shrub. Leaves grayish-green. Flowers pink, red, or white, in cymes of up to 80. Prune annually in spring by deadheading, and to maintain symmetry.

- Evergreen
- Poisonous
- Requires space
- Skin irritant

Osteospermum 'Buttermilk' A.G.M. (Asteraceae)

Common name: None
Height: 2ft (60cm)
Spread: 2ft (60cm)
Aspect: Sun
Soil: Well-drained, humus-rich
Hardiness: Zone 9
Propagation: Softwood cuttings in spring; semi-ripe cuttings in summer
Flowering time: Late spring to autumn

An evergreen subshrub. Flowers daisy-like, with primrose ray florets, and dark mauve disc florets. Usually treated as an annual.

- Evergreen
- Good cut flower
- Highly allergenic
- Must deadhead
- Prone to mildew

Osteospermum caulescens (= 'White Pim') A.G.M.

Osteospermum 'Nairobi Purple'

Osteospermum 'Whirligig' A.G.M.

Pachystachys lutea A.G.M.

Osteospermum caulescens (= 'White Pim')
A.G.M. (Asteraceae)

Common name: None
Height: 4in (10cm)
Spread: 2ft (60cm)
Aspect: Full sun
Soil: Well-drained, humus-rich
Hardiness: Zone 8
Propagation: Seed in heat in spring
Flowering time: Late spring to autumn

A prostrate, evergreen subshrub. Flowers
daisy-like, solitary, white, with gray centers.
Deadheading is all the pruning required.

* Evergreen
* Highly allergenic
* Must deadhead

Osteospermum 'Nairobi Purple'
(Asteraceae)

Common name: None
Height: 6in (15cm)
Spread: 3ft (90cm)
Aspect: Full sun
Soil: Well-drained, humus-rich
Hardiness: Zone 8
Propagation: Softwood cuttings in spring;
semi-ripe cuttings in summer
Flowering time: Late spring to autumn

A sprawling, evergreen subshrub. Flowers
daisy-like, solitary, single, purple, with black
centers. Deadheading prolongs flowering.
Usually treated as an annual.

* Evergreen
* Highly allergenic
* Must deadhead

Osteospermum 'Whirligig' A.G.M.
(Asteraceae)

Common name: None
Height: 2ft (60cm)
Spread: 2ft (60cm)
Aspect: Full sun
Soil: Well-drained, humus-rich
Hardiness: Zone 8
Propagation: Softwood cuttings in spring;
semi-ripe cuttings in summer
Flowering time: Late spring to autumn

A sprawling, evergreen subshrub. Flowers
single, solitary daisies, with crimped ray
florets of purple or white, and dark blue
centers. Deadheading prolongs flowering.

* Good cut flower
* Evergreen
* Highly allergenic
* Must deadhead

Pachystachys lutea A.G.M. (Acanthaceae)

Common name: None
Height: 3ft (90cm)
Spread: 30in (75cm)
Aspect: Full sun
Soil: Moist, well-drained, fertile
Hardiness: Zone 10
Propagation: Softwood cuttings with bottom
heat, in summer
Flowering time: Spring and summer

An erect, evergreen shrub. Flowers tubular,
two-lipped, white, with yellow bracts, in
long, terminal spikes. Deadhead, and prune
for shape, after flowering.

* Evergreen

115

Penstemon isophyllus A.G.M.

Penstemon isophyllus A.G.M. (Scrophulariaceae)

Common name: None
Height: 28in (70cm)
Spread: 18in (45cm)
Aspect: Sun or part shade
Soil: Well-drained, fertile
Hardiness: Zone 9
Propagation: Seed, or division, in spring
Flowering time: Early to late summer

An evergreen subshrub. Leaves purple-tinged. Flowers tubular, red, in one-sided racemes. Deadhead after flowering.

- Evergreen
- Handsome foliage
- Low allergen
- Attracts slugs
- Must deadhead
- Prone to mildew

Pentas lanceolata

Pentas lanceolata (Rubiaceae)

Common name: None
Height: 6ft (1.8m)
Spread: 3ft (90cm)
Aspect: Full sun
Soil: Well-drained, fertile
Hardiness: Zone 10
Propagation: Seed in heat in spring; softwood cuttings at any time
Flowering time: Spring to autumn

An evergreen subshrub. Leaves hairy, glossy-green. Flowers in domed corymbs, long-tubed, pink, white, blue, or lilac. Prune in spring by deadheading and to keep size and symmetry.

- Evergreen
- Handsome foliage

Pericallis lanata 'Kew' form (Asteraceae)

Common name: None
Height: 3ft (90cm)
Spread: 1ft (30cm)
Aspect: Sun (but not midday), or part shade
Soil: Well-drained, fertile
Hardiness: Zone 9
Propagation: Seed in heat in spring/summer; semi-ripe cuttings in summer
Flowering time: Winter to late summer

A subshrub from Tenerife. Leaves 5–7-lobed, mid-green. Scented flowers, solitary or in corymbs, daisy-like, ray florets mauve, disc florets purple.

- Scented flowers

Phlomis fruticosa A.G.M. (Lamiaceae)

Common name: None
Height: 4ft (1.2m)
Spread: 5ft (1.5m)
Aspect: Sun
Soil: Well-drained, fertile
Hardiness: Zone 7
Propagation: Seed in heat, in spring; softwood cuttings in summer
Flowering time: Early and midsummer

An evergreen subshrub. Leaves gray-green. Flowers deadnettle-like, yellow, in whorls. Prune annually after flowering by deadheading and for shape.

- Can be dried
- Drought-tolerant
- Evergreen
- Good cut flower
- Handsome foliage

Pericallis lanata 'Kew' variety

Phlomis fruticosa A.G.M.

Phygelius aequalis

Phygelius aequalis 'Sensation' (PBR)

Phygelius aequalis (Scrophulariaceae)

Common name: None
Height: 3ft (90cm)
Spread: 3ft (90cm)
Aspect: Sun
Soil: Moist, well-drained, fertile
Hardiness: Zone 8
Propagation: Suckers, soft woodcuttings, or seed, in spring
Flowering time: All summer

A half-hardy, evergreen shrub. Flowers long tubular, pendent, pink with yellow throats, in panicles. Prune in spring, by cutting back hard or by deadheading and for shape.

● Evergreen   ● Invasive

Phygelius aequalis 'Sensation' (PBR) (Scrophulariaceae)

Common name: None
Height: 4ft (1.2m)
Spread: 3ft (90cm)
Aspect: Sun
Soil: Moist, well-drained, fertile
Hardiness: Zone 8
Propagation: Separate suckers, or softwood cuttings, in spring
Flowering time: Summer to autumn

A half-hardy, evergreen subshrub. Flowers long, tubular, cerise, in panicles. Prune in spring by cutting back hard, or by deadheading, as required.

● Evergreen   ● Invasive

Phygelius aequalis 'Yellow Trumpet' A.G.M.

Phygelius aequalis 'Yellow Trumpet' A.G.M. (Scrophulariaceae)

Common name: None
Height: 4ft (1.2m)
Spread: 3ft (90cm)
Aspect: Sun
Soil: Moist, well-drained, fertile
Hardiness: Zone 8
Propagation: Separate suckers, or softwood cuttings, in spring
Flowering time: All summer

A half-hardy, evergreen, suckering subshrub. Flowers long, tubular, yellow, in panicles. Prune in spring, by cutting back hard, or by deadheading and pruning for shape.

● Evergreen   ● Invasive

Phygelius x *rectus*

Phygelius x *rectus* (Scrophulariaceae)

Common name: None
Height: 4ft (1.2m)
Spread: 4ft (1.2m)
Aspect: Sun
Soil: Moist, well-drained, fertile
Hardiness: Zone 8
Propagation: Separate suckers, or take softwood cuttings in spring
Flowering time: Most of the summer

An evergreen, suckering, subshrub. Flowers long, tubular, pale red, in panicles. Prune in spring either by cutting back hard, or by deadheading, as required.

● Evergreen   ● Invasive

Phygelius x *rectus* 'Moonraker'

Phygelius x *rectus* 'Moonraker'
(**Scrophulariaceae**)

Common name: None
Height: 5ft (1.5m)
Spread: 5ft (1.5m)
Aspect: Sun
Soil: Moist, well-drained, fertile
Hardiness: Zone 8
Propagation: Separate suckers, or take softwood cuttings, in spring
Flowering time: Most of the summer

An evergreen, suckering subshrub. Flowers long, tubular, creamy-yellow, in panicles. Prune in spring by cutting back hard, or deadheading and pruning for shape.

- Evergreen
- Invasive
- Requires space

Plumbago auriculata **A.G.M.**
(**Plumbaginaceae**)

Common name: None
Height: 20ft (6m)
Spread: 10ft (3m)
Aspect: Full sun
Soil: Well-drained, fertile
Hardiness: Zone 9
Propagation: Seed in heat in spring; semi-ripe cuttings with bottom heat in summer
Flowering time: Summer to late autumn

A large, evergreen, climbing shrub. Flowers long-tubed, sky blue, in dense racemes. Prune in early spring by cutting back to within 3 or 4 buds of permanent framework.

- Evergreen
- Requires space

Plumeria alba (**Apocynaceae**)

Common name: None
Height: 20ft (6m)
Spread: 12ft (4m)
Aspect: Full sun
Soil: Well-drained, fertile
Hardiness: Zone 10
Propagation: Seed in heat or ripe cuttings of leafless stem tips in spring
Flowering time: Summer to autumn

A large, deciduous shrub. Flowers salverform, white, with yellow eyes. Pruning is minimal, except to maintain shape and size.

-
- Scented flowers
- Poisonous

Plumbago auriculata A.G.M.

Plumeria alba

Plumeria rubra (**Apocynaceae**)

Common name: None
Height: 22ft (7m)
Spread: 15ft (4.5m)
Aspect: Full sun
Soil: Well-drained, fertile
Hardiness: Zone 10
Propagation: Seed in heat, or ripe cuttings of leafless stem tips, in spring
Flowering time: Summer to late autumn

A large, deciduous shrub. Flowers salverform, rose-pink, with yellow eyes. Minimal pruning required, except for shape and size. Superb specimen plant.

- Scented flowers
- Poisonous
- Requires space

Plumeria rubra

Polygala myrtifolia (Polygalaceae)

Common name: None
Height: 8ft (2.5m)
Spread: 6ft (1.8m)
Aspect: Sun or part shade
Soil: Sharply-drained, humus-rich, fertile
Hardiness: Zone 9
Propagation: Seed in heat in spring
Flowering time: Spring to autumn, or longer

A large, evergreen shrub. Flowers pink-purple, in short, terminal racemes. Pruning is minimal: deadhead, and cut out shoots which spoil symmetry.

• Evergreen   • Requires space

Potentilla fruticosa 'Abbotswood' A.G.M.
(Rosaceae)

Common name: Bush cinquefoil
Height: 3ft (90cm)
Spread: 5ft (1.5m)
Aspect: Sun
Soil: Well-drained
Hardiness: Zone 2
Propagation: Greenwood cuttings in early summer
Flowering time: Late spring to mid-autumn

A hardy, deciduous shrub. Leaves dark green. Flowers flat, white, in cymes. Prune in spring by cutting back flowered shoots to within 1in (2.5cm) of previous year's growth.

• Attracts bees   • Requires space
• Low allergen

Potentilla fruticosa 'Goldfinger' A.G.M.
(Rosaceae)

Common name: Bush cinquefoil
Height: 4ft (1.2m)
Spread: 4ft (1.2m)
Aspect: Sun
Soil: Well-drained
Hardiness: Zone 2
Propagation: Greenwood cuttings in early summer
Flowering time: Late spring to mid-autumn

A hardy, deciduous shrub. Flowers flat, rich yellow, in cymes. Prune in spring by cutting back flowered shoots to within 1in (2.5cm) of previous year's growth.

• Attracts bees
• Low allergen

Potentilla fruticosa 'Pretty Polly'
(Rosaceae)

Common name: Bush cinquefoil
Height: 20in (50cm)
Spread: 30in (75cm)
Aspect: Sun
Soil: Well-drained
Hardiness: Zone 2
Propagation: Greenwood cuttings in early summer
Flowering time: Late spring to mid-autumn

A dwarf, hardy, deciduous shrub. Flowers flat, pale pink, in cymes. Prune in spring by cutting back flowered shoots to within 1in (2.5cm) of previous year's growth.

• Attracts bees
• Low allergen

Polygala myrtifolia

Potentilla fruticosa 'Abbotswood' A.G.M.

Potentilla fruticosa 'Goldfinger' A.G.M.

Potentilla fruticosa 'Pretty Polly'

119

Punica granatum flore plena A.G.M. (Punicaceae)

Common name: None
Height: 20ft (6m)
Spread: 15ft (4.5m)
Aspect: Full sun
Soil: Well-drained, fertile
Hardiness: Zone 9
Propagation: Seed in heat in spring; semi-ripe cuttings, with bottom heat, in summer
Flowering time: Long period in summer

A large, deciduous shrub. Leaves glossy-green. Flowers double funnels, orange-red, followed by edible fruits. Prune (if wall-trained) by cutting back to within 2–4 buds of permanent framework; if not, prune wayward shoots out after flowering.

• Handsome foliage   • Requires space

Rhodanthemum hosmariense A.G.M. (Asteraceae)

Common name: None
Height: 1ft (30cm)
Spread: 1ft (30cm)
Aspect: Sun
Soil: Sharply-drained, fertile
Hardiness: Zone 8
Propagation: Seed in spring; softwood cuttings in early summer
Flowering time: Early spring to autumn; all year in warmth

A sprawling subshrub. Leaves intensely silver. Flowers daisy-like, single, solitary, white, with yellow centers and silver bracts.

• Drought-tolerant   • Highly allergenic
• Handsome foliage

Romneya coulteri A.G.M. (Papaveraceae)

Common name: Matilija-poppy
Height: 8ft (2.5m)
Spread: Indefinite
Aspect: Full sun
Soil: Well-drained, fertile
Hardiness: Zone 7
Propagation: Seed when ripe; division in spring
Flowering time: Long period in summer

A tall, invasive, deciduous subshrub. Leaves glaucous gray-green. Flowers solitary, scented, large single cups, white with yellow centers.

• Handsome foliage   • Invasive
• Scented flowers   • Requires space
                    • Requires staking

Rhodanthemum hosmariense A.G.M.

ROSA (Rosaceae)
Rose

A genus of about 150 species of deciduous shrubs and climbers. They can be subdivided into old-fashioned and modern categories, and the members of the latter group can be either long-flowering or repeat-flowering (remontant). Roses prefer a position in sun, but will tolerate some shade. They prefer soil to be moist but well-drained, and rich in humus. It is not advisable to dig up old plants and replace them with new stock without first digging out the old soil and replacing it with fresh.

Roses are best planted during winter or early spring. Most roses have been grafted onto wild rose rootstock, and it is important not to bury the grafted area, as suckers are the more likely to appear: these are shoots from the rootstock and must be cut out. Many modern roses are registered by trademark, and/or protected by Plant Breeders Rights, and such varieties are indicated by ®, ™ or (PBR) in the text captions.

Roses are prone to a battery of diseases, pests, insects, and ruminants, and the reader is referred to specialist texts for details of these, and their prevention and cure.

Punica granatum flore plena A.G.M.

Rosa 'Ballerina' A.G.M.

Common name: None
Height: 5ft (1.5m)
Spread: 4ft (1.2m)
Aspect: Sun
Soil: Moist, well-drained, humus-rich, fertile
Hardiness: Zone 6
Propagation: Bud in summe; hardwood cuttings in autumn
Flowering time: Summer to autumn

A modern polyantha shrub rose. Flowers single, pale pink, with white centers, in large rounded clusters. Prune in late summer by cutting back to up to a third, as required.

• Good cut flower   • Prone to mildew

Rosa 'Ballerina' A.G.M.

Romneya coulteri A.G.M.

Rosa banksiae 'Lutea' A.G.M.

Common name: Banks rose
Height: 40ft (12m)
Spread: 20ft (6m)
Aspect: Sun
Soil: Moist, well-drained, humus-rich, fertile
Hardiness: Zone 6
Propagation: Bud in summer; hardwood cuttings in autumn
Flowering time: Late spring and early summer

A climbing, banksian species rose. Scented flowers, double, yellow, in clusters. In first 2 years, cut out dead wood and side shoots. After that, cut out a third of flowered stems at base after flowering.

- Good cut flower
- Low allergen
- Scented flowers
- Prone to mildew
- Requires space

Rosa 'Blue Moon' ®

Common name: None
Height: 3ft (90cm)
Spread: 28in (70cm)
Aspect: Sun
Soil: Moist, well-drained, humus-rich, fertile
Hardiness: Zone 7
Propagation: Bud in summer; hardwood cuttings in autumn
Flowering time: Summer to autumn

A large-flowered, modern bush (hybrid tea) rose. Flowers scented, double, lilac-mauve. Prune in late winter or early spring by cutting back main stems to within 10in (25cm) of the ground.

- Good cut flower
- Low allergen
- Scented flowers
- Prone to mildew

Rosa 'Charles de Mills' A.G.M.

Common name: None
Height: 5ft (1.5m)
Spread: 5ft (1.5m)
Aspect: Sun
Soil: Moist, well-drained, humus-rich, fertile
Hardiness: Zone 5
Propagation: Bud in summer; hardwood cuttings in autumn
Flowering time: All summer

An old-fashioned, thornless, Gallica rose. Flowers scented, fully double, magenta. Prune in late summer by cutting back main stems by a third, and side shoots by two-thirds.

- Good cut flower
- Low allergen
- Scented flowers
- Needs space
- Prone to mildew

Rosa 'Compassion' ® A.G.M.

Common name: None
Height: 10ft (3m)
Spread: 8ft (2.5m)
Aspect: Sun
Soil: Moist, well-drained, humus-rich, fertile
Hardiness: Zone 7
Propagation: Bud in summer
Flowering time: Summer to autumn

A modern climbing rose with double, scented, salmon-pink flowers. Prune in first 2 years only to cut out dead wood; thereafter, cut main stems back in winter or early spring to desired height, and side shoots by two-thirds.

- Good cut flower
- Low allergen
- Scented flowers
- Needs space
- Prone to mildew

Rosa banksiae 'Lutea' A.G.M.

Rosa 'Blue Moon' ®

Rosa 'Compassion' ® A.G.M.

Rosa 'Charles de Mills' A.G.M.

Rosa 'De Rescht' A.G.M.

Common name: None
Height: 4ft (1.2m)
Spread: 3ft (90cm)
Aspect: Sun
Soil: Moist, well-drained, humus-rich, fertile
Hardiness: Zone 5
Propagation: Bud in summer
Flowering time: All summer

An old, Damask Portland rose. Flowers double, deep purple-pink. Prune main stems back lightly, or by up to one third, just after flowering.

- Good cut flower
- Low allergen
- Scented flowers
- Prone to mildew

Rosa 'Double Delight' ®

Common name: None
Height: 3ft (90cm)
Spread: 2ft (60cm)
Aspect: Sun
Soil: Moist, well-drained, humus-rich, fertile
Hardiness: Zone 7
Propagation: Bud in summer
Flowering time: Summer to autumn

A modern, large-flowered bush (hybrid tea) rose. Flowers double, scented, pale pink, margined red. Prune in late winter/early spring by cutting back main stems to within 10in (25cm) of the ground.

- Good cut flower
- Low allergen
- Scented flowers
- Prone to mildew

Rosa 'Elina' A.G.M. ® (PBR)

Common name: None
Height: 4ft (1.2m)
Spread: 30in (75cm)
Aspect: Sun
Soil: Moist, well-drained, humus-rich, fertile
Hardiness: Zone 7
Propagation: Bud in summer
Flowering time: Summer to autumn

A modern, large-flowered bush (hybrid tea) rose. Flowers scented, double, ivory-colored, with lemon centers. Prune in late winter/early spring by cutting back main stems to within 10in (25cm) of the ground.

- Good cut flower
- Low allergen
- Scented flowers
- Prone to mildew

Rosa 'Ena Harkness'

Common name: None
Height: 15ft (4.5m)
Spread: 3ft (90cm)
Aspect: Sun
Soil: Moist, well-drained, humus-rich, fertile
Hardiness: Zone 7
Propagation: Bud in summer
Flowering time: Summer to autumn

A vigorous climbing rose with scented, double, pendent, crimson flowers. In the first 2 years, cut out dead wood; thereafter, prune main shoots back to the desired height, and side shoots by two thirds.

- Good cut flower
- Low allergen
- Scented flowers
- Prone to mildew

Rosa 'Double Delight' ®

Rosa 'Elina' A.G.M. ® (PBR)

Rosa 'De Rescht' A.G.M.

Rosa 'Ena Harkness'

Rosa 'Flower Carpet' A.G.M. (PBR)

Common name: None
Height: 30in (75cm)
Spread: 4ft (1.2m)
Aspect: Sun
Soil: Moist, well-drained, humus-rich, fertile
Hardiness: Zone 4
Propagation: Bud in summer
Flowering time: Summer to autumn

A robust, ground-cover rose. Flowers double, dark rose-pink, in clusters, borne freely. Prune in late winter/spring by cutting back to outward-facing buds at levels to suit size requirements.

- Low allergen
- Prone to mildew

Rosa 'Fragrant Cloud'

Common name: None
Height: 30in (75cm)
Spread: 2ft (60cm)
Aspect: Sun
Soil: Moist, well-drained, humus-rich fertile
Hardiness: Zone 7
Propagation: Bud in summer
Flowering time: Summer to autumn

A compact, large-flowered (hybrid tea) bush rose. Flowers double, highly-scented, dusky scarlet. Prune in late winter/early spring by cutting back to within 10in (25cm) of the ground.

- Good cut flower
- Prone to mildew
- Low allergen
- Scented flowers

Rosa 'Fred Loads' A.G.M.

Common name: None
Height: 6ft (1.8m)
Spread: 3ft (90cm)
Aspect: Sun
Soil: Moist, well-drained, humus-rich, fertile
Hardiness: Zone 7
Propagation: Bud in summer
Flowering time: Summer to autumn

A robust, cluster-flowered, polyantha bush rose. Flowers vermilion-orange, in many-flowered clusters. Prune in late winter/early spring by cutting back to within 10in (25cm) of the ground.

- Good cut flower
- Prone to mildew
- Low allergen

Rosa 'Fulton Mackay' (PBR)

Common name: None
Height: 30in (75cm)
Spread: 2ft (60cm)
Aspect: Sun
Soil: Moist, well-drained, humus-rich, fertile
Hardiness: Zone 7
Propagation: Bud in summer
Flowering time: Summer to autumn

A compact, large-flowered (hybrid tea) bush rose. Flowers double, scented, apricot, flushed pink. Prune in late winter/early spring by cutting back to within 10in (25cm) of the ground.

- Good cut flower
- Prone to mildew
- Low allergen
- Scented flowers

Rosa 'Fragrant Cloud'

Rosa 'Fred Loads' A.G.M.

Rosa 'Flower Carpet' A.G.M. (PBR)

Rosa 'Fulton Mackay' (PBR)

Rosa 'Gertrude Jekyll' A.G.M. ® (PBR)

Common name: None
Height: 4ft (1.2m)
Spread: 3ft (90cm)
Aspect: Sun
Soil: Moist, well-drained, humus-rich, fertile
Hardiness: Zone 7
Propagation: Bud in summer
Flowering time: Summer to autumn

A large-flowered shrub rose. Flowers scented, double, pink. Prune back main stems by up to a third, and side shoots by two-thirds or as required, after flowering.

- Good cut flower
- Prone to mildew
- Low allergen
- Scented flowers

Rosa 'Gertrude Jekyll' A.G.M. ® (PBR)

Rosa 'Golden Wedding' (PBR)

Rosa 'Golden Wedding' (PBR)

Common name: None
Height: 3ft (90cm)
Spread: 2ft (60cm)
Aspect: Sun
Soil: Moist, well-drained, humus-rich, fertile
Hardiness: Zone 5
Propagation: Bud in summer
Flowering time: Summer to autumn

A large-flowered, bush (hybrid tea) rose. Flowers double, yellow. Prune in spring by cutting back to within 10in (25cm) of the ground.

- Good cut flower
- Prone to mildew
- Low allergen

Rosa 'Golden Wings' A.G.M.

Rosa 'Gordon's College' (PBR)

Rosa 'Golden Wings' A.G.M.

Common name: None
Height: 4ft (1.2m)
Spread: 5ft (1.5m)
Aspect: Sun
Soil: Moist, well-drained, humus-rich, fertile
Hardiness: Zone 4
Propagation: Bud in summer
Flowering time: Summer to autumn

A spreading shrub rose. Flowers single cups, scented, pale yellow. Prune main stems back by up to a third, and side shoots by two-thirds, after flowering.

- Good cut flower
- Prone to mildew
- Low allergen
- Requires space
- Scented flowers

Rosa 'Gordon's College' (PBR)

Common name: None
Height: 3ft (90cm)
Spread: 2ft (60cm)
Aspect: Sun
Soil: Moist, well-drained, humus-rich, fertile
Hardiness: Zone 5
Propagation: Bud in summer
Flowering time: Summer to autumn

A large-flowered floribunda rose. Flowers rich pink. Very disease-resistant. Prune in spring by cutting back to within 10in (25cm) of the ground.

- Good cut flower
- Low allergen

Rosa 'Happy Times'

Rosa 'Joseph's Coat'

Rosa 'Happy Times' (Rosaceae)

Common name: None
Height: 1ft (30cm)
Spread: 1ft (30cm)
Aspect: Sun
Soil: Moist, well-drained, humus-rich, fertile
Hardiness: Zone 5
Propagation: Bud in summer
Flowering time: Summer to autumn

A dwarf, miniature, bush rose. Flowers rich pink, in clusters. Prune by cutting back main stems by up to a third, and side stems by two-thirds, after flowering.

- Good cut flower
- Prone to mildew
- Low allergen

Rosa 'Joseph's Coat' (Rosaceae)

Common name: None
Height: 4ft (1.2m)
Spread: 3ft (90cm)
Aspect: Sun
Soil: Moist, well-drained, fertile
Hardiness: Zone 4
Propagation: Bud in summer
Flowering time: Summer to autumn

A robust shrub or climbing rose. Flowers double, yellow suffused pink, in clusters. Prune main stems by up to a third, and side stems by up to two-thirds, after flowering.

- Good cut flower
- Prone to mildew
- Low allergen

Rosa 'Lady MacRobert'

Rosa 'Lady MacRobert'

Common name: None
Height: 4ft (1.2m)
Spread: 3ft (90cm)
Aspect: Sun
Soil: Moist, well-drained, humus-rich, fertile
Hardiness: Zone 4
Propagation: Bud in summer
Flowering time: Summer to autumn

A cluster-flowered (floribunda) bush rose Flowers double, pink, with cream centers. Prune in late winter or early spring by cutting back to within 10in (25cm) of the ground.

- Good cut flower
- Prone to mildew
- Low allergen

Rosa 'Lavender Lassie' A.G.M.

Common name: None
Height: 4ft (1.2m)
Spread: 3ft (90cm)
Aspect: Sun
Soil: Moist, well-drained, humus-rich, fertile
Hardiness: Zone 5
Propagation: Bud in summer
Flowering time: Summer to autumn

A hybrid musk rose. Flowers scented, double, medium-sized, pink, in clusters. Prune in spring by cutting back to within 10in (25cm) of the ground.

- Good cut flower
- Prone to mildew
- Low allergen
- Scented flowers

Rosa 'Lavender Lassie' A.G.M.

126

Rosa 'Mme. Isaac Pereire' A.G.M.   *Rosa* 'National Trust'

Rosa 'Oranges and Lemons' (PBR)

Rosa 'Paul Ricault'

Rosa 'Mme. Isaac Pereire' A.G.M.

Common name: None
Height: 7ft (2m)
Spread: 6ft (1.8m)
Aspect: Sun
Soil: Moist, well-drained, humus-rich, fertile
Hardiness: Zone 7
Propagation: Bud in summer
Flowering time: Summer to autumn

A robust, bourbon shrub or climbing rose. Flowers double, scented, deep pink. Prune in late winter/early spring by cutting back main stems by a third, and side shoots by two-thirds.

- Good cut flower
- Low allergen
- Scented flowers
- Prone to mildew
- Requires space

Rosa 'National Trust'

Common name: None
Height: 2ft (60cm)
Spread: 2ft (60cm)
Aspect: Sun
Soil: Moist, well-drained, humus-rich, fertile
Hardiness: Zone 7
Propagation: Bud in summer
Flowering time: Summer to autumn

A dwarf, large-flowered bush (hybrid tea) rose. Flowers double, scarlet, borne freely. Prune back by up to within 10in (25cm) of the ground in late winter or early spring.

- Good cut flower
- Low allergen
- Prone to mildew

Rosa 'Oranges and Lemons' (PBR)

Common name: None
Height: 32in (80cm)
Spread: 2ft (60cm)
Aspect: Sun
Soil: Moist, well-drained, fertile, humus-rich
Hardiness: Zone 6
Propagation: Bud in summer
Flowering time: Summer to autumn

A robust, cluster-flowered (floribunda) bush rose. Flowers double, orange, striped scarlet, fading to pinkish-red. Prune in late winter to early spring by cutting back to within 18in (45cm) of the ground.

- Low allergen
- Good cut flower
- Prone to mildew

Rosa 'Paul Ricault'

Common name: None
Height: 5ft (1.5m)
Spread: 4ft (1.2m)
Aspect: Sun
Soil: Moist, well-drained, humus-rich, fertile
Hardiness: Zone 7
Propagation: Bud in summer
Flowering time: Summer to autumn

A hybrid perpetual rose; habit arching and lax. Flowers double, scented, deep pink. Prune back in late winter/early spring to within 10in (25cm) of the ground.

- Good cut flower
- Low allergen
- Scented flowers
- Prone to mildew

127

Rosa 'Pink Grootendorst' A.G.M.

Rosa 'Queen Mother' A.G.M (PBR)

Rosa 'Samaritan' (PBR)

Rosa 'Warm Wishes' (PBR)

Rosa 'Pink Grootendorst' A.G.M.

Common name: None
Height: 5ft (1.5m)
Spread: 3ft (90cm)
Aspect: Sun
Soil: Moist, well-drained, humus-rich, fertile
Hardiness: Zone 3
Propagation: Bud in summer
Flowering time: Summer to autumn

An upright, dense, Rugosa rose. Flowers double, rose-pink, in crowded clusters. Prune main shoots by cutting back, after flowering, by up to one third, and side shoots by up to two-thirds.

- Good cut flower
- Low allergen
- Prone to mildew

Rosa 'Queen Mother' A.G.M (PBR)

Common name: None
Height: 16in (40cm)
Spread: 2ft (60cm)
Aspect: Sun
Soil: Moist, well-drained, fertile, humus-rich
Hardiness: Zone 6
Propagation: Bud in summer
Flowering time: Summer to autumn

A dwarf, cluster-flowered (floribunda) bush patio rose. Flowers flat, clear pink. Prune in late winter to early spring by cutting back main stems and side shoots by up to a half.

- Good cut flower
- Low allergen
- Prone to mildew

Rosa 'Samaritan' (PBR)

Common name: None
Height: 28in (70cm)
Spread: 2ft (60cm)
Aspect: Sun
Soil: Moist, well-drained, humus-rich, fertile
Hardiness: Zone 7
Propagation: Bud in summer
Flowering time: Summer to autumn

A large-flowered bush (hybrid tea) rose. Flowers double, scented, pink, ageing to red, in wide sprays. Prune in early spring by cutting back to within 10in (25cm) of the ground.

- Good cut flower
- Low allergen
- Scented flowers
- Prone to mildew

Rosa 'Warm Wishes' (PBR)

Common name: None
Height: 3ft (90cm)
Spread: 2ft (60cm)
Aspect: Sun
Soil: Moist, well-drained, humus-rich, fertile
Hardiness: Zone 5
Propagation: Bud in summer
Flowering time: Summer to autumn

A large-flowered bush (hybrid rea) rose. Flowers double, scented, peach-pink. Prune in spring by cutting back to within 10in (25cm) of the ground.

- Good cut flower
- Low allergen
- Scented flowers
- Prone to mildew

Rosa 'William Quarrier' (PBR)

Senecio vira-vira A.G.M.

Solanum laciniatum

Solanum rantonnetti

Rosa 'William Quarrier' (PBR)

Common name: None
Height: 3ft (90cm)
Spread: 2ft (60cm)
Aspect: Sun
Soil: Moist, well-drained, humus-rich, fertile
Hardiness: Zone 6
Propagation: Bud in summer
Flowering time: Summer to autumn

A cluster-flowered (polyantha) bush rose.
Flowers large, peach-colored, in clusters.
Prune in late winter to early spring by
cutting back to within 10in (25cm) of the
ground.

- Good cut flower
- Low allergen
- Prone to mildew

Senecio vira-vira A.G.M. (Asteraceae)

Common name: None
Height: 2ft (60cm)
Spread: 3ft (90cm)
Aspect: Sun
Soil: Sharply-drained, fertile
Hardiness: Zone 6
Propagation: Seed in spring; semi-ripe
cuttings in summer
Flowering time: Summer to autumn

An evergreen subshrub. Leaves ferny, gray-
green. Flowers composed only of disc
florets, off-white, in loose corymbs. Prune
by deadheading, and to maintain shape.

- Attracts bees
- Evergreen
- Handsome foliage
- Highly allergenic
- Poisonous

Solanum laciniatum (Solanaceae)

Common name: None
Height: 6ft (1.8m)
Spread: 5ft (1.5m)
Aspect: Sun
Soil: Alkaline, moist, well-drained, fertile
Hardiness: Zone 9
Propagation: Semi-ripe cuttings with bottom
heat in summer
Flowering time: Summer to autumn

A robust, evergreen shrub. Leaves
pinnatisect, mid-green. Flowers dark blue,
in axillary cymes. Prune by deadheading,
and cutting back shoots which spoil
symmetry, in spring.

- Evergreen
- Handsome foliage
- Poisonous
- Requires space

Solanum rantonnetti (Solanaceae)

Common name: Paraguay nightshade
Height: 6ft (1.8m)
Spread: 6ft (1.8m)
Aspect: Sun
Soil: Alkaline, moist, well-drained, fertile
Hardiness: Zone 9
Propagation: Semi-ripe cuttings with bottom
heat in summer
Flowering time: Summer to mid-autumn

An evergreen shrub. Leaves shiny green.
Flowers violet-blue saucers, in axillary
clusters. Prune by deadheading, and cutting
out shoots which spoil symmetry, in
spring.

- Evergreen
- Handsome foliage
- Poisonous
- Requires space

Spiraea japonica 'Goldflame' A.G.M. (Rosaceae)

Common name: Japanese spirea
Height: 30in (75cm)
Spread: 30in (75cm)
Aspect: Sun
Soil: Moist, well-drained, fertile
Hardiness: Zone 5
Propagation: Greenwood cuttings in summer
Flowering time: Mid- and late summer

A deciduous shrub. Leaves yellow, turning green. Flowers bowl-shaped, pink, in terminal corymbs. Prune annually, after flowering, by cutting back 25% of shoots to the base.

● Low allergen

Spiraea japonica 'Goldflame' A.G.M.

Spiraea japonica 'Shirobana' A.G.M.

Spiraea japonica 'Shirobana' A.G.M. (Rosaceae)

Common name: Japanese spirea
Height: 2ft (60cm)
Spread: 2ft (60cm)
Aspect: Sun
Soil: Moist, well-drained, fertile
Hardiness: Zone 5
Propagation: Greenwood cuttings in summer
Flowering time: Mid- to late summer

A deciduous shrub. Flowers bowl-shaped, pink and white at the same time, in terminal corymbs. Prune annually after flowering by cutting back 25% of stems to the base.

● Low allergen

Streptosolen jamesonii A.G.M.

Streptosolen jamesonii A.G.M. (Solanaceae)

Common name: Orange streptosolen
Height: 10ft (3m)
Spread: 8ft (2.5m)
Aspect: Sun
Soil: Moist, well-drained, fertile
Hardiness: Zone 9
Propagation: Softwood cuttings, with bottom heat in early summer
Flowering time: Late spring to late summer

A large evergreen, semi-scandent shrub. Flowers tubular, orange-yellow, in large terminal corymbs. Deadhead after flowering, and prune in spring for size and shape.

● Evergreen   ● Requires space

Tweedia caerulea A.G.M. (Asclepiadaceae)

Common name: None
Height: 3ft (90cm)
Spread: 8in (20cm)
Aspect: Sun
Soil: Moist, well-drained, fertile
Hardiness: Zone 10
Propagation: Seed in spring; softwood cuttings in summer
Flowering time: Summer to early autumn

An erect, twining, evergreen subshrub. Flowers sky-blue, ageing to purple, in few-flowered cymes. Prune in spring by cutting back flowered shoots to within 2–4 buds of permanent framework.

● Good cut flower

Tweedia caerulea A.G.M.

Verbascum 'Letitia' A.G.M.
(Scrophulariaceae)

Common name: None
Height: 10in (25cm)
Spread: 1ft (30cm)
Aspect: Sun
Soil: Sharply-drained poor
Hardiness: Zone 7
Propagation: Division in spring; root cuttings in winter
Flowering time: Summer to autumn

A dwarf, evergreen subshrub. Leaves gray-green. Flowers flat, yellow, with reddish centers, in short racemes.

- Attracts bees
- Drought-tolerant
- Evergreen
- Handsome foliage
- Prone to mildew

Viburnum tinus (Caprifoliaceae)

Common name: Laurestinus viburnum
Height: 10ft (3m)
Spread: 10ft (3m)
Aspect: Sun or part shade
Soil: Moist, well-drained, fertile
Hardiness: Zone 7
Propagation: Semi-ripe cuttings in summer
Flowering time: Late winter and early spring

An evergreen shrub. Flowers small, salveriform, white, in flattened, terminal cymes. Minimal pruning required, but will tolerate being cut hard back.

- Evergreen
- Poisonous
- Requires space

Vinca major 'Variegata' A.G.M.
(Apocynaceae)

Common name: Big periwinkle
Height: 18in (45cm)
Spread: Indefinite
Aspect: Sun or part shade
Soil: Humus rich, moisture retentive
Hardiness: Zone 7
Propagation: Division, between autumn and spring
Flowering time: Spring to summer

A prostrate evergreen shrub, but which can be tied into an upright position. Foliage green, margined cream. Flowers star-shaped, lilac-blue. Can be cut back in early spring.

- Evergreen
- Handsome foliage
- Invasive
- Poisonous

Verbascum 'Letitia' A.G.M.

Vinca minor 'Alba Variegata' (Apocynaceae)

Common name: Periwinkle, Myrtle
Height: 8in (20cm)
Spread: Indefinite
Aspect: Sun or part shade
Soil: Humus-rich, moisture-retentive
Hardiness: Zone 4
Propagation: Division, from autumn to spring
Flowering time: Spring to summer

A prostrate, evergreen shrub. Leaves margined cream. Flowers white. Can be cut back in early spring as necessary.

- Evergreen
- Handsome foliage
- Invasive
- Poisonous

Viburnum tinus

Vinca major 'Variegata' A.G.M.

Vinca minor 'Alba Variegata'

SECTION THREE
ANNUALS

———— ✳ ————

A plant that flowers, sets seed, and dies in a single season is termed an annual, whereas a plant that makes leaf in its first season, then flowers, sets seed, and dies in the second season is a biennial. Both are conventionally classified as hardy or half-hardy, and their culture is handled differently.

Hardy annuals can withstand frost and can be sown *in situ* in autumn. If treated like a biennial and sown in autumn for flowering the next season, annuals will flower much earlier and bloom much longer than if they are sown in early spring. Half-hardly annuals can only be sown when all danger of frost is past and as a result flowering will be comparatively late and short-lived. In order to ensure half-hardy annuals have a long flowering season, they must be sown in heat in late winter or early spring and planted out after the last frost.

The terms 'annual' and 'biennial' are sometimes erroneously assumed to be synonymous with 'bedding plant' but many tender perennials bloom in their first year from seed and are handled as if they were annuals. These three categories of plant are all grouped together as bedding plants, and can be grown in beds or borders exclusive to them; this method of display was common in Victorian times and is again popular today.

Many bedding plants require frequent deadheading if long flowering is to be attained, otherwise they will set seed and cease flowering. The Common snapdragon, *Antirrhinum majus*, is one popular bedding plant that must be deadheaded on a regular basis if it is to be kept flowering; on the other hand the Sultan snapweed, *Impatiens walleriana*, is an example of a plant that will remain flowering without.

Bedding plants are used extensively to cover gaps left by early flowering plants in beds and borders, and are also the mainstay of containers and hanging baskets. They will continue to flower well into the winter, or if planted up with perennials they may flower all winter provided the containers are taken into a warm environment before the plants have been exposed to a first frost.

Ageratum houstonianum (Asteraceae)

Common name: None
Height: 18in (45cm)
Spread: 1ft (30cm)
Aspect: Full sun
Soil: Moist, well-drained
Hardiness: Zone 8
Propagation: Seed in heat in spring
Flowering time: Midsummer to first frost

A compact, mound-forming annual. Leaves oval, downy, dull green. Flowers in panicles, of up to 40, blue, pink or white. Deadheading prolongs flowering.

● Highly allergenic
● Must deadhead

Amberboa moschata (Asteraceae)

Common name: None
Height: 2ft (60cm)
Spread: 10in (25cm)
Aspect: Full sun
Soil: Well-drained, fertile
Hardiness: Zone 8
Propagation: Seed in spring
Flowering time: Spring to summer

A branching annual. Basal leaves entire, stem leaves pinnatifid, gray-green. Flowers scented, cornflower-like, on erect stems. Color varies from white and yellow to pink or purple.

● Good cut flower
● Must deadhead
● Prone to mildew
● Requires staking

Anchusa capensis (Boraginaceae)

Common name: None
Height: 7in (18cm)
Spread: 5in (12cm)
Aspect: Full sun
Soil: Well-drained, humus-rich
Hardiness: Zone 9
Propagation: Seed in heat in spring
Flowering time: All summer

An erect annual or biennial. Leaves narrow lance-shaped, rough, mid-green. Flowers open saucers in panicles, bright blue with a white throat.

● Attracts bees
● Low allergen

Argemone mexicana (Papaveraceae)

Common name: Mexican prickle-poppy
Height: 3ft (90cm)
Spread: 16in (40cm)
Aspect: Full sun
Soil: Sharply-drained, poor
Hardiness: Zone 8
Propagation: Seed in heat in early spring
Flowering time: Late summer to autumn

A clump-forming annual from southern U.S.A. and Central America. Leaves elliptic, deeply-lobed, silver-veined, blue-green, very spiny. Flowers solitary, scented, poppy-like, yellow.

● Drought-tolerant
● Handsome foliage
● Must deadhead
● Seeds everywhere

Ageratum houstonianum

Amberboa moschata

Anchusa capensis

Argemone mexicana

Borago officinalis

Bracteantha bracteata Monstrosum group

Calceolaria Herbeohybrida group

Brachycome iberidifolia

Borago officinalis (Boraginaceae)

Common name: Common borage
Height: 2ft (60cm)
Spread: 18in (45cm)
Aspect: Sun or part shade
Soil: Well-drained
Hardiness: Zone 7
Propagation: Seed *in situ* in spring
Flowering time: Long period in summer

A strongly-growing, branching annual with basal and stem leaves; the former are ovate, bristly, dull green, the latter are lance-shaped. The flowers are in branched cymes, star-shaped, 5-petaled, blue. Deadhead to prevent seeding.

- Prone to mildew
- Seeds everywhere

Brachycome iberidifolia (Asteraceae)

Common name: Swan River daisy
Height: 18in (45cm)
Spread: 15in (38cm)
Aspect: Full sun
Soil: Well-drained, fertile
Hardiness: Zone 8
Propagation: Seed in heat in spring
Flowering time: All summer

A spreading annual from Australia. Leaves pinnatisect, downy gray-green. Flowers are scented and may be white, purple, or blue. Deadheading prolongs flowering.

- Drought-tolerant
- Scented flowers
- Attracts slugs
- Must deadhead

Bracteantha bracteata Monstrosum group (Asteraceae)

Common name: None
Height: 5ft (1.5m)
Spread: 1ft (30cm)
Aspect: Full sun
Soil: Moist, well-drained
Hardiness: Zone 8
Propagation: Seed in heat in spring
Flowering time: Late spring to autumn

A perennial from Australia, grown universally as an annual. Leaves lance-shaped, gray-green. Flowers solitary, terminal, papery, in a color range of white, yellow, pink, or red.

- Can be dried
- Highly allergenic
- Short-lived

Calceolaria Herbeohybrida group (Scrophulariaceae)

Common name: None
Height: 18in (45cm)
Spread: 1ft (30cm)
Aspect: Sun or part shade
Soil: Acid, gritty, fertile
Hardiness: Zone 9
Propagation: Seed, surface-sown, in spring or late summer
Flowering time: All summer

Compact biennials. Leaves ovate, hairy, mid-green. Flowers in cymes of up to 15, yellow, orange, or bicolored. Excellent in baskets.

- Attracts slugs

135

Calendula officinalis

Callistephus chinensis

Campanula medium

Centaurea cyanus 'Diadem'

Calendula officinalis (Asteraceae)

Common name: Pot marigold
Height: 28in (70cm)
Spread: 18in (45cm)
Aspect: Sun or part shade
Soil: Any, but well-drained
Hardiness: Zone 6
Propagation: Seed in spring
Flowering time: Midsummer to autumn

An annual with inverse lance-shaped, aromatic, hairy, leaves of mid-green. Flowers daisy-like, double or single, in yellow, orange, apricot, or cream, borne profusely.

- Aromatic foliage
- Drought-tolerant
- Highly allergenic
- Must deadhead
- Prone to mildew

Callistephus chinensis (Asteraceae)

Common name: China aster
Height: 2ft (60cm)
Spread: 18in (45cm)
Aspect: Full sun
Soil: Moist, well-drained, fertile
Hardiness: Zone 8
Propagation: Seed in heat in early spring
Flowering time: Late summer to autumn

A monotypic genus of annual. Leaves ovate, toothed, mid-green. Flowers single or double, like chrysanthemums, in all shades.

- Good cut flower

Campanula medium (Campanulaceae)

Common name: Canterbury bells
Height: 3ft (90cm)
Spread: 1ft (30cm)
Aspect: Sun or part shade
Soil: Well-drained, fertile
Hardiness: Zone 8
Propagation: Seed in autumn or spring
Flowering time: Spring to summer

A very popular biennial. Leaves basal, lance-shaped, mid-green. Flowers in racemes, bell-shaped, single or double, in white, pink, or blue. Will repeat-flower if sheared over after flowering.

- Good cut flower
- Attracts slugs

Centaurea cyanus 'Diadem' (Asteraceae)

Common name: Cornflower
Height: 30in (75cm)
Spread: 6in (15cm)
Aspect: Full sun
Soil: Well-drained
Hardiness: Zone 7
Propagation: Seed *in situ* in spring or autumn
Flowering time: Late spring to midsummer

An upright annual. Leaves lance-shaped, entire, mid-green. Flowers deep blue.

- Good cut flower
- Highly allergenic
- Must deadhead
- Must not be moved

Cerinthe major 'Purpurascens'

Cerinthe major 'Purpurascens'
(Boraginaceae)

Common name: Honeywort
Height: 18in (45cm)
Spread: 1ft (30cm)
Aspect: Sun
Soil: Well-drained
Hardiness: Zone 7
Propagation: Seed in spring
Flowering time: March onwards

An annual from the Mediterranean area.
Leaves heart-shaped, blue-green, blotched
white when young. Flowers tubular, green,
yellow, or purple, blue underneath, and
surrounded by blue bracts.

● Handsome foliage   ● Seeds everywhere

Chrysanthemum carinatum (Asteraceae)

Common name: Tricolor chrysanthemum
Height: 2ft (60cm)
Spread: 1ft (30cm)
Aspect: Sun
Soil: Well-drained, fertile
Hardiness: Zone 8
Propagation: Seed in spring
Flowering time: Summer to autumn

An annual from Morocco. Leaves succulent,
pinnatisect, bright green. Flowers single,
solitary, daisy-like in red, yellow, and white,
surrounding a central dark disc.

● Good cut flower   ● Attracts slugs
                      ● Must deadhead

Chrysanthemum coronarium (Asteraceae)

Common name: None
Height: 32in (80cm)
Spread: 32in (80cm)
Aspect: Full sun
Soil: Well-drained, fertile
Hardiness: Zone 7
Propagation: Seed in spring
Flowering time: Spring to summer

An annual from the Mediterranean. Leaves
ferny, pale green. Flowers single, daisy-like,
pale cream to white.

● Good cut flower   ● Attracts slugs
                      ● Must deadhead

Chrysanthemum carinatum

Chrysanthemum coronarium

Clarkia amoena (Portulacaceae)

Common name: None
Height: 30in (75cm)
Spread: 1ft (30cm)
Aspect: Sun or part shade
Soil: On the acid side, fertile, well-drained
Hardiness: Zone 10
Propagation: Seed *in situ* in spring
Flowering time: All summer

A robust annual from California. Leaves
lance-shaped, toothed, mid-green. Flowers
single or double, funnel-shaped, paper-thin, in
pastel shades, in clusters on long leafy shoots.

● Good cut flower   ● Must not be moved

Clarkia amoena

Cleome hassleriana

Consolida ajacis

Cosmos bipinnatus Sonata series A.G.M. (1)

Cosmos bipinnatus Sonata series A.G.M. (2)

Cleome hassleriana (Capparidaceae)

Common name: Spiderflower
Height: 5ft (1.5m)
Spread: 18in (45cm)
Aspect: Full sun
Soil: Sharply-draining, fertile
Hardiness: Zone 10
Propagation: Seed in heat in spring
Flowering time: All summer, if deadheaded

An erect annual. Stems hairy. Leaves 5/7-palmate, hairy, toothed, mid-green. Flowers scented, spider-like, white, pink, or purple, in dense terminal racemes.

- Drought-tolerant
- Good cut flower
- Scented flowers
- Highly allergenic
- Must deadhead

Consolida ajacis (Ranunculaceae)

Common name: Larkspur
Height: 4ft (1.2m)
Spread: 1ft (30cm)
Aspect: Full sun
Soil: Well-drained, fertile
Hardiness: Zone 10
Propagation: Seed in situ in spring
Flowering time: All summer

A little- to well-branched annual with finely dissected fern-like foliage. Flowers single or double, spurred, in upright spikes, open to densely-packed, in pastel or rich shades of violet, blue, pink, or white.

- Can be dried
- Good cut flower
- Handsome foliage
- Attracts slugs
- Poisonous
- Prone to mildew

Cosmos bipinnatus Sonata series A.G.M. (Asteraceae) (1)

Common name: Common cosmos
Height: 4ft (1.2m)
Spread: 18in (45cm)
Aspect: Full sun
Soil: Moist, well-drained, fertile
Hardiness: Zone 10
Propagation: Seed in heat in spring
Flowering time: All summer, if deadheaded

An erect annual, with pinnatisect mid-green leaves. Flowers solitary, saucer-shaped, deep red with yellow centers.

- Handsome foliage
- Highly allergenic
- Must deadhead

Cosmos bipinnatus Sonata series A.G.M. (Asteraceae) (2)

Common name: Common cosmos
Height: 4ft (1.2m)
Spread: 18in (45cm)
Aspect: Full sun
Soil: Moist, well-drained, fertile
Hardiness: Zone 10
Propagation: Seed in heat in spring
Flowering time: All summer, if deadheaded

An annual with ferny foliage. Flowers solitary, saucer-shaped, pink, with yellow centers.

- Handsome foliage
- Highly allergenic
- Must deadhead

Cynoglossum amabile A.G.M. (Boraginaceae)

Common name: Chinese forget-me-not
Height: 2ft (60cm)
Spread: 1ft (30cm)
Aspect: Sun or part shade
Soil: Moist, well-drained
Hardiness: Zone 7
Propagation: Seed *in situ* in mid-spring
Flowering time: Late summer

A bushy, upright, slow-growing annual or biennial. Leaves gray-green, hairy, obovate. Flowers sky blue, in one-sided terminal cymes.

- Handsome foliage
- Must not be moved

Dimorphotheca sinuata (Asteraceae)

Common name: Winter Cape-marigold
Height: 1ft (30cm)
Spread: 1ft (30cm)
Aspect: Full sun
Soil: Well-drained, fertile, open
Hardiness: Zone 9
Propagation: Seed in heat in spring
Flowering time: Summer to autumn

An erect annual from South Africa. Leaves coarsely-toothed, aromatic. Flowers on stiff stems, single, solitary, in yellow, orange, white, or pink, with a brown-violet center.

- Aromatic foliage
- Good cut flower
- Must deadhead

Dorotheanthus bellidiformis (Aizoaceae)

Common name: None
Height: 6in (15cm)
Spread: 1ft (30cm)
Aspect: Full sun
Soil: Sharply-drained, poor
Hardiness: Zone 9
Propagation: Seed in heat in early spring
Flowering time: All summer

A colorful, low-growing annual. Leaves fleshy, cylindrical, glistening, green. Flowers single, solitary, daisies in a myriad of colors, but open only in sunshine.

- Drought-tolerant
- Handsome foliage
- Attracts slugs

Echium vulgare 'Dwarf Bedder' (Boraginaceae)

Common name: Common viper's bugloss
Height: 3ft (90cm)
Spread: 1ft (30cm)
Aspect: Full sun
Soil: Well-drained, fertile
Hardiness: Zone 7
Propagation: Seed in spring, or in autumn for the next year
Flowering time: All summer, if deadheaded

An upright, compact biennial. Leaves white-hairy. Flowers bell-shaped, with a prominent green calyx, in shades of pink, blue, or white.

- Attracts slugs
- Must deadhead

Cynoglossum amabile A.G.M.

Dimorphotheca sinuata

Dorotheanthus bellidiformis

Echium vulgare 'Dwarf Bedder'

Eschscholzia californica A.G.M.
(Papaveraceae)

Common name: Californian poppy
Height: 1ft (30cm)
Spread: 6in (15cm)
Aspect: Full sun
Soil: Well-drained
Hardiness: Zone 6
Propagation: Seed *in situ* in spring
Flowering time: Many weeks in summer

A hardy annual with finely-divided leaves of
gray-green. Flowers single, usually orange,
but which may be white, yellow, or red.

● Drought-tolerant
● Good cut flower
● Handsome foliage

Eustoma grandiflorum (Gentianaceae)

Common name: Russell prairie-gentian
Height: 3ft (90cm)
Spread: 1ft (30cm)
Aspect: Full sun
Soil: Well-drained, fertile
Hardiness: Zone 9
Propagation: Seed in heat in autumn or
early spring
Flowering time: All summer

An annual from south U.S.A. Leaves glaucous
gray-green. Flowers wide bells, lilac or white,
with dark centers. For the hot dry garden.

● Good cut flower   ● Prone to mildew
● Handsome foliage

Felicia bergeriana (Asteraceae)

Common name: Kingfisher-daisy
Height: 10in (25cm)
Spread: 10in (25cm)
Aspect: Full sun
Soil: Well-drained
Hardiness: Zone 9
Propagation: Seed in heat in spring
Flowering time: All summer and early
autumn

A tender annual from South Africa. Leaves
hairy, gray-green. Flowers solitary, single,
blue daisies, with yellow centers, open only
in sunshine. Good in hot, dry gardens.

● Handsome foliage   ● Highly allergenic

Eschscholzia californica A.G.M.

Gaillardia pulchella (Asteraceae)

Common name: Painted gaillardia
Height: 18in (45cm)
Spread: 1ft (30cm)
Aspect: Full sun
Soil: Well-drained
Hardiness: Zone 8
Propagation: Seed in heat in spring, or in
situ in early summer
Flowering time: Summer to autumn

An upright annual from south U.S.A. and
Mexico. Flowers have red, yellow, or red/
yellow, ray florets, and purple disc florets.

● Drought-tolerant   ● Attracts slugs
● Good cut flower   ● Highly allergenic
                       ● Must deadhead

Eustoma grandiflorum

Gaillardia pulchella

Felicia bergeriana

Helianthus annuus

Helianthus annuus (Asteraceae)

Common name: Common sunflower
Height: 15ft (5m)
Spread: 2ft (60cm)
Aspect: Full sun
Soil: Moist, humus-rich, fertile
Hardiness: Zone 10
Propagation: Seed in heat in late winter, or in situ in spring
Flowering time: All summer

A very tall, fast-growing annual. Leaves rough, hairy, dark green. Flowers large, solitary or branched, single or double, single- or multicolored in yellow or red. Never allow seedlings to dry out. Seeds are edible.

- Attract bees
- Good cut flower
- Attracts slugs
- Prone to mildew
- Skin irritant

Iberis umbellulata 'Fantasia' (Brassicaceae)

Common name: Globe candytuft
Height: 1ft (30cm)
Spread: 10in (25cm)
Aspect: Sun
Soil: Well-drained, fertile
Hardiness: Zone 7
Propagation: Seed *in situ* in spring
Flowering time: Spring to summer

A bushy annual. Flowers scented, small, in flattened corymbs, in a range of colors.

- Low allergen
- Scented flowers
- Attracts slugs
- Must deadhead
- Must not be moved

Impatiens balfourii (Balsaminaceae)

Common name: None
Height: 3ft (90cm)
Spread 1ft (30cm)
Aspect: Sun or part shade
Soil: Moist, well-drained, humus-rich
Hardiness: Zone 10
Propagation: Seed, in heat, in early spring
Flowering time: Summer to early autumn

A tender annual. Flowers bicolored, white and rich mauve.

- Seeds everywhere

Impatiens glandulifera (Balsaminaceae)

Common name: None
Height: 6ft (1.8m)
Spread 2ft (60cm)
Aspect: Shade
Soil: Moist,
Hardiness: Zone 10
Propagation: Seed in spring
Flowering time: Midsummer to mid-autumn

A weed of woods and waste places. Flowers scented, red, rose, lavender, or white, interior spotted yellow. Seed capsules explosive.

- Scented flowers
- Seeds everywhere

Iberis umbellulata 'Fantasia'

Impatiens balfourii

Impatiens glandulifera

141

Ipomoea purpurea

Lavatera trimestris

Lupinus texensis

Ipomoea purpurea (Convolvulaceae)

Common name: None
Height: 10ft (3m)
Spread: 3ft (90cm)
Aspect: Full sun
Soil: Well-drained, fertile
Hardiness: Zone 7
Propagation: Seed in heat in spring
Flowering time: Long periods in summer

An annual, twining climber. Flowers trumpet-shaped, purple, blue, pink, or white, or white striped with these colors, in cymes.

- Prone to mildew

Lathyrus odoratus 'Winston Chuchill' A.G.M. (Papilionaceae)

Common name: Sweet pea
Height: 6ft (1.8m)
Spread: 2ft (60cm)
Aspect: Sun or light shade
Soil: Well-drained, humus-rich, fertile
Hardiness: Zone 5
Propagation: Seed, after soaking, in autumn, or spring
Flowering time: Summer to early autumn

An annual that needs little introduction. Leaves dark green, stems winged. Flowers on long stems, scented, in all colors (except yellow) or bicolored. Seeds poisonous.

- Good cut flower
- Scented flowers
- Attracts slugs
- Must deadhead
- Poisonous
- Prone to mildew

Lavatera trimestris (Malvaceae)

Common name: Herb tree-mallow
Height: 5ft (1.5m)
Spread: 5ft (1.5m)
Aspect: Sun
Soil: Well-drained, fertile
Hardiness: Zone 8
Propagation: Seed *in situ* in late spring
Flowering time: All summer

Bushy annual with solitary, open, funnel-shaped flowers in pink, rose-red, or white.

- Drought-tolerant
- Good cut flower
- Must not be moved

Limnanthes douglasii A.G.M.

Limnanthes douglasii A.G.M. (Limnanthaceae)

Common name: Meadow-foam
Height: 6in (15cm)
Spread: 2ft (60cm)
Aspect: Sun
Soil: Moist, well-drained, fertile
Hardiness: Zone 8
Propagation: Seed *in situ* in spring or autumn
Flowering time: Summer to autumn

A half-hardy annual. Leaves toothed, glossy. Flowers yellow cups with white centers.

- Attracts bees
- Scented flowers
- Must not be moved

Lupinus texensis (Papilionaceae)

Common name: None
Height: 1ft (30cm)
Spread: 10in (25cm)
Aspect: Sun
Soil: Sharply-drained
Hardiness: Zone 9
Propagation: Seed in spring or autumn
Flowering time: All summer, if deadheaded

A bushy, upright annual. Flowers in dense racemes, deep blue or purple. Seeds poisonous.

- Drought-tolerant
- Attracts slugs
- Must deadhead
- Poisonous

Lathyrus odoratus 'Winston Chuchill' A.G.M.

Mentzelia lindleyi

Nemesia strumosa 'Carnival' series

Mentzelia lindleyi (Loasaceae)

Common name: Lindley mentzelia
Height: 28in (70cm)
Spread: 10in (25cm)
Aspect: Full sun
Soil: Well-drained, fertile
Hardiness: Zone 9
Propagation: Seed *in situ* in spring
Flowering time: Early to late summer

A tender annual for the hot, dry garden.
Leaves pinnatifid, gray-green. Flowers night-
scented, solitary, or in few-flowered cymes,
yellow with orange centers. Cut hard back
to get second flush of flowers.

● Handsome foliage
● Scented flowers

Nemesia strumosa 'Carnival' series (Scrophulariaceae)

Common name: Pouch nemesia
Height: 1ft (30cm)
Spread: 6in (15cm)
Aspect: Full sun
Soil: Acidic, moist, well-drained
Hardiness: Zone 9
Propagation: Seed in heat in spring
Flowering time: Mid- to late summer

A strain of compact, dwarf habit. Flowers in
a range of colors, with darker veins and pale
throats, in terminal racemes.

● Good cut flower

Nemesia strumosa 'K.L.M.' strain

Nemesia strumosa 'K.L.M.' strain (Scrophulariaceae)

Common name: Pouch nemesia
Height: 1ft (30cm)
Spread: 6in (15cm)
Aspect: Sun
Soil: Acidic, moist, well-drained, fertile
Hardiness: Zone 9
Propagation: Seed in heat in spring
Flowering time: Early to late summer

A strain of compact, dwarf habit. Flowers
two-lipped, bicolored, in terminal racemes.

● Good cut flower

Nemesia strumosa 'National Ensign' strain (Scrophulariaceae)

Common name: Pouch nemesia
Height: 1ft (30cm)
Spread: 6in (15cm)
Aspect: Sun
Soil: Acidic, moist, well-drained
Hardiness: Zone 9
Propagation: Seed in heat in spring
Flowering time: Early to late summer

A strain of compact, dwarf habit. Flowers
two-lipped, bicolored, in terminal racemes.

● Good cut flower

Nemesia strumosa 'National Ensign' strain

Nicandra physaloides 'Violacea' (Solanaceae)

Common name: Apple-of-Peru
Height: 3ft (90cm)
Spread: 1ft (30cm)
Aspect: Full sun
Soil: Moist, well-drained, fertile
Hardiness: Zone 8
Propagation: Seed in heat in spring
Flowering time: Summer to autumn

An upright, half-hardy annual. Flowers short-lived, bell-shaped, pale violet-blue, with white centers in the upper leaf axils, followed by brown berries.

● Seeds everywhere

Nicotiana 'Domino Lime Green' A.G.M. (Solanaceae)

Common name: None
Height: 2ft (60cm)
Spread: 10in (25cm)
Aspect: Sun or half shade
Soil: Moist, well-drained, fertile
Hardiness: Zone 7
Propagation: Seed in heat, in spring
Flowering time: All summer

An upright, hardy annual. Flowers lime green, salveriform, borne abundantly.

● Scented flowers   ● Skin irritant

Nicotiana langsdorfii A.G.M. (Solanaceae)

Common name: None
Height: 5ft (1.5m)
Spread: 15in (38cm)
Aspect: Sun or part shade
Soil: Moist, well-drained, fertile
Hardiness: Zone 9
Propagation: Seed in heat in spring
Flowering time: Long periods in summer

A tall, tender, sticky annual. Leaves in a basal rosette. Flowers tubular, nodding, apple-green, in tall, slender panicles.

● Scented flowers   ● Skin irritant

Nigella damascena 'Miss Jekyll' A.G.M (Ranunculaceae)

Common name: Love-in-a-mist
Height: 20in (50cm)
Spread: 10in (25cm)
Aspect: Full sun
Soil: Well-drained
Hardiness: Zone 10
Propagation: Seed *in situ* in spring
Flowering time: All summer

An upright annual with very finely-divided green leaves. Flowers terminal on tall stems, sky blue, and surrounded by a ruff of foliage.

● Handsome foliage   ● Must not be moved

Nigella hispanica 'Curiosity' (Ranunculaceae)

Common name: None
Height: 30in (75cm)
Spread: 18in (45cm)
Aspect: Sun
Soil: Well-drained
Hardiness: Zone 10
Propagation: Seed *in situ* in spring
Flowering time: Long periods in summer

An upright annual with finely-divided, ferny foliage. Flowers terminal on tall stems, solitary or paired, scented, bright blue, with black eyes and deep red stamens.

● Handsome foliage   ● Must not be moved
● Scented flowers

Nicandra physaloides 'Violacea'

Nicotiana 'Domino Lime Green' A.G.M.

Nigella damascena 'Miss Jekyll' A.G.M

Nicotiana langsdorfii A.G.M.

Nigella hispanica 'Curiosity'

Oenothera biennis (Onagraceae)

Common name: Common evening-primrose
Height: 5ft (1.5m)
Spread: 2ft (60cm)
Aspect: Full sun
Soil: Sharply-drained
Hardiness: Zone 4
Propagation: Seed in early summer for next season
Flowering time: Summer to autumn

A tall annual, grown usually as a biennial. Leaves in a basal rosette. Flowers bowl-shaped, scented, pale yellow darkening to deep yellow, in leafy racemes.

- Drought-tolerant
- Scented flowers
- Attracts slugs

Onopordum acanthium (Asteraceae)

Common name: None
Height: 10ft (3m)
Spread: 3ft (90cm)
Aspect: Sun
Soil: Well-drained, fertile
Hardiness: Zone 6
Propagation: Seed in autumn or spring
Flowering time: Several weeks in summer

A very tall, tap-rooted, rosette-forming biennial. Leaves spiny, gray-green. Flowers thistle-like, purple, surrounded by spiny bracts.

- Handsome foliage
- Attracts slugs
- Seeds everywhere

Papaver commutatum A.G.M. (Papaveraceae)

Common name: None
Height: 18in (45cm)
Spread: 6in (15cm)
Aspect: Full sun
Soil: Well-drained, fertile
Hardiness: Zone 8
Propagation: Seed in spring
Flowering time: Several weeks in summer

An annual upright, branched poppy. Flowers solitary, bright scarlet, with black basal spots.

- Drought-tolerant
- Low allergen
- Must not be moved
- Prone to mildew
- Seeds everywhere

Papaver dubium (Papaveraceae)

Common name: None
Height: 2ft (60cm)
Spread: 8in (20cm)
Aspect: Sun
Soil: Well-drained, fertile
Hardiness: Zone 7
Propagation: Seed in spring
Flowering time: All summer

An upright, angular, hairy annual, with pinnatisect leaves of blue-green. Flowers solitary, single, pale red or pink.

- Drought-tolerant
- Handsome foliage
- Low allergen
- Seeds everywhere

Onopordum acanthium

Papaver commutatum A.G.M.

Papaver dubium

Oenothera biennis

Phacelia campanularia

Phlox drummondii 'Beauty' series

Phlox drummondii 'Dolly' series

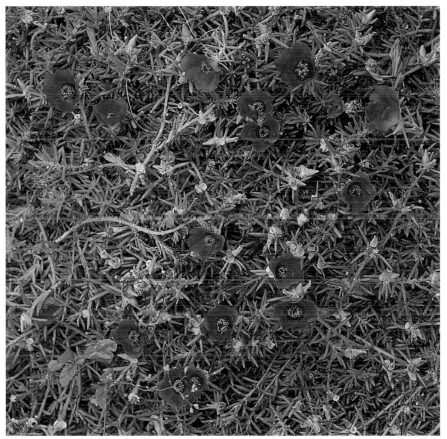

Portulaca grandiflora

Phacelia campanularia (Hydrophyllaceae)

Common name: Harebell phacelia
Height: 1ft (30cm)
Spread: 6in (15cm)
Aspect: Full sun
Soil: Well-drained, fertile
Hardiness: Zone 9
Propagation: Seed in situ in spring
Flowering time: Spring to summer

An upright annual. Leaves aromatic.
Flowers upward-facing, dark blue bells.

• Attracts bees   • Skin irritant

Phlox drummondii 'Beauty' series (Polemoniaceae)

Common name: Annual/Drummond phlox
Height: 9in (23cm)
Spread: 10in (25cm)
Aspect: Full sun
Soil: Well-drained, fertile
Hardiness: Zone 6
Propagation: Seed in heat in early spring
Flowering time: Late spring to autumn

An erect or spreading, bushy annual. Flowers salveriform, white, red, pink, blue, or purple, with contrasting basal markings, in cymes.

• Low allergen   • Prone to mildew

Phlox drummondii 'Dolly' series (Polemoniaceae)

Common name: Annual/Drummond phlox
Height: 6in (15cm)
Spread: 6in (15cm)
Aspect: Full sun
Soil: Well-drained, fertile
Hardiness: Zone 6
Propagation: Seed in heat in spring
Flowering time: Late spring to late summer

A dwarf clone of bushy, hardy annuals. Flowers salveriform, single-colored or bicolored, in a range of colors, in cymes.

• Low allergen   • Prone to mildew

Portulaca grandiflora (Portulacaceae)

Common name: Sunplant, Common portulaca
Height: 8in (20cm)
Spread: 6in (15cm)
Aspect: Full sun
Soil: Sharply-drained, poor
Hardiness: Zone 10
Propagation: Seed in heat in spring
Flowering time: All summer

A prostrate annual. Leaves narrow, cylindrical, fleshy. Flowers single or double, pink, red, orange, yellow, or white. For hot dry gardens.

• Drought-tolerant
• Handsome foliage

Salpiglossis sinuata 'Casino' series A.G.M.

Schizanthus pinnatus

Silybum marianum

Senecio elegans

Salpiglossis sinuata 'Casino' series A.G.M. (Solanaceae)

Common name: Painted-tongue
Height: 2ft (60cm)
Spread: 1ft (30cm)
Aspect: Full sun
Soil: Moist, well-drained, humus-rich
Hardiness: Zone 8
Propagation: Seed in spring or autumn
Flowering time: Summer to autumn

A short-lived perennial, grown almost always as an annual. Flowers funnel-shaped, solitary, in a wide range of colors, and sometimes heavily-veined. For the hot, dry garden.

● Good cut flower   ● Must deadhead

Sanvitalia procumbens (Asteraceae)

Common name: Trailing sanvitalia
Height: 8in (20cm)
Spread: 18in (45cm)
Aspect: Sun
Soil: Humus-rich, well-drained, fertile
Hardiness: Zone 7
Propagation: Seed *in situ* in autumn or spring
Flowering time: Summer to early autumn

A sprawling, hardy annual. Flowers single, daisy-like, yellow, with black centers. Good in hanging baskets.

● Highly allergenic
● Must not be moved

Sanvitalia procumbens

Schizanthus pinnatus (Solanaceae)

Common name: Butterfly-flower
Height: 20in (50cm)
Spread: 1ft (30cm)
Aspect: Sun
Soil: Moist, well-drained, fertile
Hardiness: Zone 10
Propagation: Seed in heat in spring
Flowering time: Spring to autumn

An erect annual. Flowers two-lipped, in a range of colors, and spotted, open cymes. Pinch out seedlings to make bushy and dwarf.

● Good cut flower   ● Requires staking

Senecio elegans (Asteraceae)

Common name: None
Height: 2ft (60cm)
Spread: 18in (45cm)
Aspect: Sun
Soil: Well-drained
Hardiness: Zone 9
Propagation: Seed in heat in spring
Flowering time: Long period in summer

A tender annual. Flowers have red-purple ray florets and yellow disc florets, in corymbs.

● Attracts bees   ● Highly allergenic
                     ● Poisonous

Silybum marianum (Asteraceae)

Common name: None
Height: 5ft (1.5m)
Spread: 3ft (90cm)
Aspect: Sun
Soil: Well-drained
Hardiness: Zone 7
Propagation: Seed *in situ* in late spring
Flowering time: Summer to autumn, in the year after sowing

A biennial, with a basal rosette of glossy, marbled, leaves, often grown for its foliage. Flowers thistle-like, scented, purple-pink.

● Good cut flower   ● Attracts slugs
● Handsome foliage
● Scented flowers

Tagetes erecta 'Antigua' series

Tagetes patula 'Beaux' series

TAGETES *(Asteraceae)*
Marigold

A genus of only 50 species, but one which provides us with some of our most popular and widely-used annuals, derived from *Tt. patula, erecta,* and *tenuifolia.* Four principal hybrid annual types are recognized:

African marigolds, derived from *T. erecta.* These have pinnate leaves, and large, fully-double, pompon-like flowers of yellow or orange. Flowers are borne from spring to autumn. These are especially useful in formal bedding schemes.

French marigolds, derived from *T. patula.* These have pinnate leaves. The solitary, double, and occasionally single, flowers have ray florets of yellow, brown, or orange (or combinations of these). The disc florets are the same or different colors; flowering is from late spring to autumn. They are useful in the front of mixed borders.

Afro-French marigolds, derived from *Tt. erecta* and *patula.* These have pinnate leaves. The small flowers, which may be single or double, in yellow and orange, are marked red or brown. They grow in cymes or solitary, from late spring to autumn.

Signet marigolds, derived from *T. tenuifolia.* These have pinnate leaves. The single flowers are rich in disc florets of yellow or orange, but lack ray florets. Flowering is from late spring to autumn.

Marigolds like full sun and soil which is well-drained. The foliage may cause skin irritation. They are highly allergenic, and prone to attack by slugs. Marigolds require to be deadheaded to keep flowering.

Tagetes patula 'Boy' series

Tagetes erecta 'Antigua' series *(Asteraceae)*

Common name: African marigold
Height: 1ft (30cm)
Spread: 18in (45cm)
Aspect: Sun
Soil: Well-drained, fertile
Hardiness: Zone 9
Propagation: Seed *in situ* in late spring, or in heat in early spring
Flowering time: Late spring to early autumn

A strain of African marigold. Leaves ferny. Produces double flowers of yellow, orange, lemon, or primrose.

- Handsome foliage
- Attracts slugs
- Highly allergenic
- Must deadhead
- Skin irritant

Tagetes patula 'Beaux' series *(Asteraceae)*

Common name: Afro-French marigold
Height: 14in (35cm)
Spread: 18in (45cm)
Aspect: Sun
Soil: Well-drained, fertile
Hardiness: Zone 9
Propagation: Seed in heat in early, or *in situ* in late spring
Flowering time: Late spring to late summer

A compact, free-flowering Afro-French marigold. Leaves ferny. Flowers densely double, golden yellow.

- Handsome foliage
- Attracts slugs
- Highly allergenic
- Must deadhead
- Skin irritant

Tagetes patula 'Boy' series *(Asteraceae)*

Common name: French marigold
Height: 6in (15cm)
Spread: 1ft (30cm)
Aspect: Sun
Soil: Well-drained, fertile
Hardiness: Zone 9
Propagation: Seed *in situ* in late spring, or in heat in early spring
Flowering time: Late spring to autumn

A strain of compact French marigolds. Leaves ferny. Flowers large, double, of yellow, orange, or red, with yellow or orange crests.

- Handsome foliage
- Attracts slugs
- Highly allergenic
- Must deadhead
- Skin irritant

Tagetes patula 'Orange Boy' (Asteraceae)

Common name: French marigold
Height: 6in (15cm)
Spread: 1ft (30cm)
Aspect: Sun
Soil: Well-drained, fertile
Hardiness: Zone 9
Propagation: Seed in heat in early spring, or in situ in late spring
Flowering time: Late spring to late summer

A very compact, free-flowering strain. Leaves ferny. Flowers double, crested, bright orange.

- Handsome foliage
- Attracts slugs
- Highly allergenic
- Must deadhead
- Skin irritant

Tagetes tenuifolia 'Lemon Gem' (Asteraceae)

Common name: None
Height: 16in (40cm)
Spread: 18in (45cm)
Aspect: Sun
Soil: Well-drained, fertile
Hardiness: Zone 9
Propagation: Seed in heat in early spring, or in situ in late spring
Flowering time: Late spring to late summer

A compact, dwarf strain of Signet marigolds. Leaves ferny. Flowers single, lemon-yellow.

- Handsome foliage
- Attracts slugs
- Highly allergenic
- Must deadhead
- Skin irritant

Tagetes tenuifolia 'Tangerine Gem' (Asteraceae)

Common name: None
Height: 16in (40cm)
Spread: 18in (45cm)
Aspect: Sun
Soil: Well-drained, fertile
Hardiness: Zone 9
Propagation: Seed in heat in early spring, or in situ in late spring
Flowering time: Late spring to late summer

A compact, dwarf strain of Signet marigolds. Leaves ferny. Flowers single, orange with deep orange centers.

- Handsome foliage
- Attracts slugs
- Highly allergenic
- Must deadhead
- Skin irritant

Torenia fournieri 'Clown' series (Scrophulariaceae)

Common name: None
Height: 10in (25cm)
Spread: 9in (23cm)
Aspect: Part shade
Soil: Moist, well-drained, fertile
Hardiness: Zone 9
Propagation: Seed in heat in spring
Flowering time: All summer

An upright annual. Flowers tubular, flared, two-lipped, purple, lavender, white, or pink in terminal or axillary racemes.

Tagetes patula 'Orange Boy'

Tagetes tenuifolia 'Lemon Gem'

Tagetes tenuifolia 'Tangerine Gem'

Torenia fournieri 'Clown' series

Torenia fournieri 'Panda' series

Tropaeolum 'Alaska' series A.G.M.

Torenia fournieri 'Panda' series
(Scrophulariaceae)

Common name: None
Height: 8in (20cm)
Spread: 9in (23cm)
Aspect: Part shade
Soil: Moist, well-drained, fertile
Hardiness: Zone 9
Propagation: Seed in heat, in spring
Flowering time: Several weeks in summer

An erect annual. Flowers tubular, flared,
two-lipped, purple, pink, white, or lavender,
in terminal or axillary racemes.

Tropaeolum 'Alaska' series A.G.M.
(Tropaeolaceae)

Common name: None
Height: 1ft (30cm)
Spread: 18in (45cm)
Aspect: Sun
Soil: Poor, well-drained
Hardiness: Zone 8
Propagation: Seed in heat in early spring, or
in situ in late spring
Flowering time: Summer to autumn

A compact, dwarf strain with leaves speckled
and marked white. Flowers single, in a
range of colors. Leaves and flowers edible.

- Handsome foliage
- Attracts slugs
- Seeds everywhere

Tropaeolum 'Empress of India'

Tropaeolum 'Empress of India'
(Tropaeolaceae)

Common name: None
Height: 1ft (30cm)
Spresd: 18in (45cm)
Aspect: Sun
Soil: Poor, well-drained
Hardiness: Zone 8
Propagation: Seed in heat in early spring, or
in situ in late spring
Flowering time: Summer to autumn

A compact, dwarf annual. Flowers semi-
double, scarlet. Leaves and flowers edible.

- Attracts slugs
- Seeds everywhere

Tropaeolum majus (Tropaeolaceae)

Common name: Common nasturtium
Height: 10ft (3m)
Spread: 15ft (4.5m)
Aspect: Sun
Soil: Poor, well-drained
Hardiness: Zone 8
Propagation: Seed in heat in early spring, or
in situ in late spring
Flowering time: Summer to autumn

A robust, annual climber or scrambler.
Flowers long-spurred, orange, red, or
yellow. Leaves and flowers edible.

- Attracts slugs
- Seeds everywhere

Zinnia elegans 'Thumbelina' series
(Asteraceae)

Common name: Common zinnia
Height: 6in (15cm)
Spread: 18in (45cm)
Aspect: Sun
Soil: Well-drained, humus-rich, fertile
Hardiness: Zone 8
Propagation: Seed in heat in early spring, or
in situ in late spring
Flowering time: Long periods in summer

A dwarf, spreading annual. Flowers single
or double, in a range of colors; weather-
resistant. Deadheading prolongs flowering.

- Highly allergenic
- Prone to mildew

Tropaeolum majus

Zinnia elegans 'Thumbelina' series

APPENDICES

Evergreen long-flowering perennials

Acanthus spinosus
Aeonium cuneatum
Anthemis punctata
Anthemis tinctoria
Bellis perennis
Calceolaria biflora
Calceolaria 'Sunset Red'
Campanula persicifolia
Catharanthus roseus
Chrysogonum virginianum
Cobaea scandens
Corydalis lutea
Eccremocarpus scaber
Erysimum linifolium
Gazania
Happlopappus glutinosus
Hemerocallis 'Corky'
Hemerocallis 'Green Flutter'
Hemerocallis 'Stafford'
Heuchera 'Red Spangles
x *Heucherella alba*
Hypericum cerastioides
Lapageria rosea
Omphalodes cappadocica
Origanum laevigatum
Osteospermum jucundum
Passiflora coerulea
Passiflora quadrangularis
Pelargonium peltatum
Pelargonium tricolor
Pelargonium zonale
Penstemon heterophyllus
Pulmonaria rubra
Pulmonaria saccharata
Thunbergia alata
Verbascum 'Helen Johnson'
Viola 'Columbine'
Viola 'Etain'
Zauschneria californica

Evergreen long-flowering shrubs

Abelia in variety
Abutilon in variety
Allamanda cathartica
Anisodontea capensis
Argyranthemum in variety
Bougainvillea glabra
Brachglottis 'Sunshine'
Bupleurum fruticosum
Caesalpinia pulcherrima
Calceolaria integrifolia
Calluna in variety
Ceanothus 'Skylark'
Ceanothus thyrsiflorus
Choisya 'Aztec Pearl'
Cistus in variety
Coronilla valentina ssp. *glauca*
Daboecia in variety
Dendromecon rigida
Erica carnea in variety
Erica cinerea in variety
Erica darleyensis in variety
Erica gracilis in variety
Erysimum 'Bowles' Mauve'
Grevillea in variety
Grindelia chiloensis
Hebe in variety
Helianthemum in variety
Hibiscus rosa-sinensis
Hypericum calycinum
Iberis sempervirens
Justicia carnea
Lavandula stoechas
Lavatera in variety
Leptospermum scoparium
Lithodora diffusa
Lupinus arboreus
Mimulus aurantiacus
Nerium oleander
Nicotiana glauca
Osteospermum in variety
Pachystachys lutea
Penstemon isophyllus
Pentas lanceolata
Phlomis fruticosa
Phygelius in variety
Plumbago auriculata
Polygala myrtifolia
Senecio vira-vira
Solanum laciniatum
Solanum rantonetti
Streptosolen jamesonii
Verbascum 'Letitia'
Viburnum tinus
Vinca major
Vinca minor

Drought-tolerant long-flowering perennials

Acanthus in variety
Alchemilla mollis
Anthemis in variety
Begonia grandis
Bracteantha 'Coco'
Calceolaria biflora
Centranthus ruber
Convolvulus althaeoides
Coreopsis vertticillata
Erigeron in variety
Eriophyllum lanatum
Erodium in variety
Erysimum in variety
Eucomis in variety
Gaillardia in variety
Gaura lindheimeri
Gazania in variety
Geranium in variety
Gypsophila in variety
Haplopappus glutinosus
Hypericum cerastioides
Limonium sinuatum
Linaria purpurea
Linum in variety
Lychnis in variety
Nepeta in variety
Nerine bowdenii
Oenothera in variety
Origanum laevigatum
Rehmannia elata
Rhodohypoxis baurii
Senecio doronicum
Sphaeralcea in variety
Stachys in variety

Drought-tolerant long-flowering shrubs

Anisodontea capensis
Bougainvillea glabra
Cistus in variety
Cytisus in variety
Erysimum in variety
Fremontodendron californicum
Grindelia chiloensis
Helianthemum in variety
Hypericum calycinum
Lavatera in variety
Phlomis fruticosa
Verbascum 'Letitia'

Drought-tolerant long-flowering annuals

Argemone mexicana
Brachycombe iberidifolia
Calendula officinalis
Cleome hassleriana
Dorotheanthus bellidiformis
Eschscholzia californica
Lavatera trimestris
Papaver dubium
Portulaca grandiflora

Low-allergen long-flowering perennials

Acanthus spinosus
Alcea rosea
Antirrhinum majus
Begonia in variety
Campanula persicifolia
Canna in variety
Clematis x *eriostemon*
Convolvulus sabatius
Convolvulus tricolor
Corydalis lutea
Cyrtanthus brachscyphus
Erodium in variety
Geranium in variety
Geum in variety
Hemerocallis in variety
Heuchera in variety
x *Heucherella alba*
Hypericum cerastiodes
Impatiens in variety
Lobelia x *gerardii*
Mimulus in variety
Monarda didyma
Nepeta in variety
Omphalodes cappadocica
Passiflora in variety
Penstemon in variety
Petunia x *hybrida*
Phlox 'Chattahoochee'
Potentilla in variety
Pulmonaria in variety
Roscoea purpurea
Salvia in variety
Scabiosa 'Irish perpetual-flowering'
Stachys byzantina
Symphytum x *uplandicum*
Tiarella wherryi
Tradescantia in variety
Veronica in variety

Viola in variety

Symphytum x *uplandicum*

Low-allergen long-flowering shrubs

Antirrhinum sempervirens
Cytisus in variety
Erica in variety
Fuchsia in variety
Hebe in variety
Helianthemum in variety
Hibiscus in variety
Hydrangea in variety
Hypericum in variety
Mimulus in variety
Penstemon in variety
Potentilla in variety
Rosa in variety
Spiraea japonica

Low-allergen long-flowering annuals

Anchusa capensis
Iberis umbellulata
Papaver commutatum
Papaver dubium
Phlox drummondii

Highly allergenic long-flowering perennials

Alstroemeria in variety
Arctotis x *hybrida*
Aster in variety
Buphthalmum salicifolium
Coreopsis in variety
Dianthus in variety
Erigeron in variety
Eriophyllum lanatum
Gaillardia in variety
Gazania in variety
Helenium in variety
Helianthus in variety
Pelargonium in variety
Rudbeckia in variety
Senecio in variety

Highly allergenic long flowering shrubs

Argyranthemum in variety
Ceanothus in variety
Euryops pectinatus
Fremontodendron californicum
Osteospermum in variety
Senecio vira-vira

Highly allergenic long-flowering annuals

Bracteantha bracteata
Calendula officinalis
Centaurea cyanus
Cleome hassleriana
Cosmos bipinnatus
Felicia bergeriana
Senecio elegans
Tagetes in variety
Zinnia elegans

Poisonous long-flowering perennials

Catharanthus roseus
Dicentra in variety
Gloriosa superba
Helenium in variety
Nerine bowdenii
Senecio in variety
Solanum in variety

Poisonous long-flowering shrubs

Brugmansia sanguinea
Cytisus in variety
Hydrangea in variety
Lantana camara
Lonicera in variety
Nerium oleander
Plumeria in variety
Senecio in variety
Solanum in variety
Vinca major
Vinca minor

Poisonous long-flowering annuals

Consolida ajacis
Lupinus in variety
Senecio elegans

BIBLIOGRAPHY

Bird, R. *The Cultivation of Hardy Perennials* Batsford, London. 1994.
Brickell, C. (Editor-in-chief) *The Royal Horticultural Society Gardeners' Encyclopaedia of Plants and Flowers* Dorling Kindersley, London. 1994.
Brickell, C. (Editor-in-chief) *The Royal Horticultural Society A-Z Encyclopaedia of Plants and Flowers* Dorling Kindersley, London. 1997.
Cooke, I. *The Plantfinder's Guide to Tender Perennials* David and Charles, Newton Abbot. 1998.
Craigmyle, M. *The Illustrated Encyclopaedia of Perennials* Salamander Books, London. 1999.
Elliott, J. *The The Smaller Perennials* Batsford, London. 1997.
Griffiths, M. *The Royal Horticultural Society Index of Garden Plants* Macmillan Press, Basingstoke. 1994.
Hessayon, D.G. *The New Bedding Plant Expert* Transworld Publishers, London. 1997.
Hessayon, D.G. *The Flowering Shrub Expert* Transworld Publishers, London. 1997.
Hessayon, D.G. *The House Plant Expert* Transworld Publishers, London. 1998.
Jellito, I., Schact, W. and Fessler, A. *Hardy Herbacious Perennials* (2 volumes) Timber Press, Portland, Oregon. 1990.
Kelly, J. (Editor) *The Hillier Gardener's Guide to Trees and Shrubs* David and Charles, Newton Abbot. 1995.
Kelly, J. (Editor) *The Royal Horticultural Society Plant Guides: Annuals and Biennials* Dorling Kindersley, London. 1999.
Kohlein, F. and Menzel, P. *The Encyclopaedia of Plants for Garden Situations* Batsford, London. 1994.
Mathew, B. and Swindells, P. *The Gardener's Guide to Bulbs* Mitchell Beazley, London. 1994.
Parker, H. (Editor) *Perennials. A Royal Horticultural Society Guide.* Dorling Kindersley, London. 1996.
Philip, C. *The Plant Finder. 2000/2001 Edition. The Royal Horticultural Society.* Dorling Kindersley, London. 19XX.
Phillips, R. and Rix, M. *Annuals and Biennials.* Pan Books, London. 1999.
Phillips, R. and Rix, M. *Bulbs.* Pan Books, London. 1989.
Phillips, R. and Rix, M. *Conservatory and Indoor Plants.* (2 volumes) Pan Books, London. 1997.
Phillips, R. and Rix, M. *Herbs.* Pan Books, London. 1990.
Phillips, R. and Rix, M. *Perennials.* (2 volumes) Pan Books, London. 1991.
Phillips, R. and Rix, M. *Shrubs.* Pan Books, London. 19XX.
Segall, B. (Consultant) *Botanica: the Illustrated A to Z of over 10,000 Garden Plants and How to Grow Them* Mynah, N.S.W., Australia. 1997.
Thomas, G.S. *Perennial Garden Plants, or the Modern Forilegium* Dent, London. 1990.
Trehane, P. et al. *International Code of Nomenclature for Garden Plants* Quarterjack Publishing, Wimborne. 1995.

INDEX

————— �֍ —————

PICTURE CREDITS

The publishers wish to thank the following photographers and picture libraries who have supplied photographs for this book. Photographs have been credited by page number and position on the page: (T) top, (B) bottom, (L) left, (R) right etc.

Harry Smith Collection: 10/11, 43(TL), 49(BR), 54(TL), 60(TL), 61(TL), 87(BL), 90(T), 92(B), 97(CL), 98(BL), 99(TL), 134(T&C), 137(TR), 144(TR&B), 146(BR), 148(CL)

Malcolm Richards/A-Z Botanical: 27(TL)

Natural Visions: 74(CR), 113(R)

Nancy Rothwell/Garden & Wildlife Matters: 134(BL)

Emap Gardening Picture Library: 148(TR)

John Glover: 151(BL)

All other photographs were taken by Professor Marshall Craigmyle.